"There's not just a gender pay gap. T.... ....
In 2013, only 19% of angel investors in the United States were women. Impact With Wings aims to close that gap, with a call to action for women to step up and invest!"

— **Jo Miller**, founding editor of BeLeaderly.com and CEO, Women's Leadership Coaching, Inc.

"Bringing together the best ideas of well-respected thought leaders in the world of angel investing for women, Wingpact has created a powerful, engaging, and highly readable book that is also a call to arms. Whether you are thinking of investing, looking for investment, or want to learn more about the history and future of women as investors, I highly recommend this book."

— **Denise Brosseau**, CEO, Thought Leadership Lab, cofounder, Springboard Enterprises

"As women achieve greater financial success, they are looking for projects they can support on behalf of women. *Impact With Wings* covers a timely topic of interest for more women than ever. It is an extremely valuable and thought-provoking narrative, coupled with practical information on financing."

— **Dr. Marsha Firestone**, president and founder, The Women Presidents' Organization

"*Impact With Wings* provides a terrific overview of why you (yes, you) should consider becoming an angel investor or entrepreneur. It covers a range of related topics including the pros and cons of crowdfunding and how certain old money patterns can hold us back and what to do about them. The authors' determination to enlist more women in providing and seeking capital will inspire you—and, fair warning, it could be life-changing."

—**Laurie Kretchmar**, Up with Social, social media marketing consultant

"Women have significant financial resources that could profoundly impact the future of women across the world. *Impact With Wings* shows us how and why, with intimate, insightful stories from real women."

—**Julie Barnes**, founder of Your Story Gold, Huffington Post Blogger, and secretary of National Association of Women Business Owners (NAWBO) Sacramento

"There is no lack of women involved in entrepreneurship. *Impact With Wings: Stories to Inspire and Mobilize Women Angel Investors and Entrepreneurs* drives that home—as well as how to drive female entrepreneurs forward. This book is a must-read for entrepreneurs, investors, and anyone interested in the future of the economy."

—**Elmira Bayrasli**, author of *From The Other Side of The World: Extraordinary Entrepreneurs, Unlikely Places* and cofounder of Foreign Policy Interrupted

"A truly inspiring book by smart, accomplished, powerful women, highlighting the benefits of investing in, and funding options for, women entrepreneurs. This is a must-read book for any woman entrepreneur looking to expand her own knowledge of funding opportunities, as well as investors who are looking for alternatives for their investment portfolio. As a Certified Financial Planner, I am excited about this time in our economy and feel confident with pioneers like the authors, the US economy will move forward in a positive way through women's entrepreneurship."

—**Brittney Castro**, CFP®, CRPC®, AAMS® and founder and CEO of Financially Wise Women

"The number of female angel investors is growing, but still lags behind the pool of male counterparts. *Impact With Wings* is a call to action for women to join the band of angel investors and is an excellent primer for entrepreneurs as it provides a blueprint for the early-stage funding process. A major impediment to women's entrepreneurial success is a lack of access to capital, and one way to increase access is to get more women involved in providing funds to disrupt the bias in today's investment landscape. 'Women helping Women' is a core tenet of The CLUB, and we applaud the authors for demystifying angel funding."

—**The CLUB**, an Incubator of Women Leaders, www.theclubsv.org

"*Impact With Wings* is what we need in order to have more women achieve entrepreneurship and invest in start-ups with multi-disciplinary teams, diversity in gender—to think big and not be afraid to fail. This book puts us in front of a reality that is sometimes less known by those who have the power to contribute to a more diverse entrepreneur ecosystem."

—**Marta Cruz**, founding partner of NXTPLabs

"As a newcomer to entrepreneurship and angel investing, this book was both inspiring and practical. Reading it gave me lots of exciting ideas and actionable resources to move me toward the next steps in my life."

—**Deborah Parker-Johnson**, cofounder, Kaleidoscope Connects and author of *Envisioning Advancement Leadership*

Impact
With
Wings

Stories to Inspire and Mobilize
Women Angel Investors
and Entrepreneurs

Dear Diann,
Soar Higher!
~ Suzanne

Impact
With
Wings

Stories to Inspire and Mobilize Women Angel Investors and Entrepreneurs

By Suzanne Andrews, Jagruti Bhikha,
Karen Bairley Kruger, Christine Emilie Lim,
Wingee Sin and Hana Yang

With Contributing Authors
Geri Stengel and Susan Preston

Green Fire Press
Housatonic, Massachusetts

Cover design by Adam Michael Rothberg
Cover concept by Christine Lim
Page design by Anna Myers Sabatini

Library of Congress Control Number: 2016934178
ISBN 978-0-9861980-2-1

Green Fire Press
PO Box 377
Housatonic, MA
01236

www.wingpact.com

This Book is Dedicated To:

Ian, Emily, and Calvin. May you design the world of your dreams. (Suzanne)

My daughters, Priya and Nisha, my nephew Bhavik and my dog, Diego—thank you for being my strength and believing in me even when I didn't. Always have kindness and love in all your actions, thoughts, and words and never give up on your dreams. Never. Ever. (Jagruti)

To Lacey, Rowan, Avery, Leia, Reeve, and all of the world's youth. Each of you is deserving of a more equal, inclusive, and compassionate world. Together we can be a part of that change. (Karen)

Royce Curtis, Reese Cayenne, and Gabriel Ray—soar higher. (Christine)

To Jacob, Wingee, Connor, Sydney, and all the children of the world. We are working on creating a more inclusive world for you to grow up in! (Wingee)

My littles, Bessie, Joshua Kyu Bum Lee, Ethan Joon Ko, Olivia Ko, Ricard Pages Yoo, and to all the children of our lives and future generations to come. (Hana)

Acknowledgments

Numerous people helped with this book from the very beginning. First, we want to acknowledge Susan Hwang, our beloved Pipeline Angels teaching assistant. We were sitting around during our last class, talking about what fun we had had and wondering why more women didn't know how powerful angel investing could be. At that point, Susan said, "You guys should write a book." That is how the idea for this book was born, and that was the spark that began Wingpact. Susan gave us the confidence that our voices were valuable and the passion to share them.

Throughout the process, we knew we wanted to include the voices of women with a vast array of experiences in the investing and entrepreneurial space. There are probably hundreds of people who spoke with us or referred us to others. Many of those conversations ended up in this book, and all of them informed our thinking and moved us ahead in some way. We have deep appreciation for all of those who shared their thinking, their dreams, and their networks.

Suzanne would like to thank the many, many women (and some men) who have opened their networks to her and included her in them. As a mother reentering the professional world, it has been deeply gratifying (and reassuring) to have opportunities to associate with and to learn from some of the most influential thinkers and innovators of our time.

Jagruti thanks her brother and sister-in-law, Pradeep and Ranjana Shah, for bringing her to this country and giving her a new beginning and an opportunity to call America her second home; her three sets of parents (yes, she is blessed to have three amazing dads and three amazing moms), her friends who are more like siblings, Mamta, Hani, and Kinnu; all her sisters, especially Aruna and Pratibha for their encouragement; Suzanne Andrews for opening the door to angel investing along with all her Wingpact cofounders; and Audrey for always accepting her for who she is. Last but not least, she thanks her daughters, Priya and Nisha, and her grandmother, Sussatie Prasad, for being sources of courage and inspiration.

Karen's deepest thanks go to Roy Richardson, Laura Payson, and Robin Dutton-Cookston, who were always abundant with support and heartfelt encouragement. And to her Wingpact colleagues, who inspire her every day to hear more voices, especially her own.

Christine thanks her parents, Emmanuelito and Cristina, for enabling her to take risks and learn from her own experiences early on in her life.

Wingee thanks Jeremy Sim for his willingness to read her very first draft and provide invaluable feedback, Ann Winblad for her words of wisdom and inspiration at the very beginning, Christine Tsai, Rui Ma, and the 500StartUp community for their remarkable work in walking the talk in diversity, the Landmark and HIVE community for their unwavering cultivation of people doing ambitious work, and Venisa, Celine, Bryce, and the Ho and Park families for providing so much love and patience, as this important work has taken time away from them.

Hana thanks her parents, Cristina Hyeyoung Yang and Roberto Kisoo Yang, for being awesome role models and parents and indefinitely believing in her throughout her adventurous life journey; her inner-circle "peeps," Andrea, Desiree, Dianne, Lilian, Natalia, Kevin, and Pato, for always being there for her no matter from which corner of the world; her partners at Manos Ventures for joining her in serving the underrepresented and diverse communities in the entrepreneurial and venture ecosystem; Miguel Casillas, Alejandro Estrada, her Kauffman Fellows, and FRB teams for encouraging and supporting her to pursue her passion in innovation investing; and her Wingpact partners for empowering her to make the world a better place.

Finally, we want to thank our miraculous editor, Audrey Kalman. She was able to take our diverse ideas and form them into a cohesive book, while reminding us that our ideas were timely and important. And a huge thank you goes to our publisher, Green Fire Press, for believing in our book from the beginning and making it real.

The Wingpact Team

Suzanne Andrews - Mother, Investor, and Global Connector

As an angel investor, Suzanne Andrews focuses her investments on women-owned positive social impact companies, with a particular interest in the fair fashion industry. Previously, as director at the Anita Borg Institute, Suzanne supported the TechWomen program, bringing technical women leaders from the Middle East and North Africa to the United States for partnerships with Silicon Valley women. From this experience, she learned about the power and opportunity in her dream of a global women's network of investors and entrepreneurs. Suzanne also writes about women's start-up culture, investigating the possibilities for disruption now that there are more women investors available to support previously underfunded high-impact women entrepreneurs. She spent ten years as a software engineer at Apple, has been a midwife's assistant and a doula, and is a proud mom to Emily, 19, and Ian, 12. Suzanne has a BA in computer science from Brown University.

Jagruti Bhikha, MS - Mom, Geek, Speaker

Jagruti Bhikha is a seasoned technical leader and strategist whose work experience includes software engineering, creating and executing programs in technology as well as conferences for women in tech, and helping to provide tech solutions for nonprofit organizations by matching tech talent with the tech needs of the nonprofit. She is currently working on a startup developing platform where women's stories are shared to support angel investors, women entrepreneurs and women in tech. She has successfully implemented Women's Entrepreneur Quest (WEQ) program in India, which is now in its fifth year and was recently featured on CNBC India. She is working to bring a similar conference program to Chile (LAtINiTY), giving women entrepreneurs an opportunity to pitch in front of government and business leaders. She currently serves as an advisor with India's most trusted platform for start-ups, LetsVenture, helping connect Indian start-ups with global angels, VCs, and start-up programs. Jagruti is passionate about women in leadership (especially tech, entrepreneurship and investing) and sharing stories of women via storiesofher.com. She holds a BS in electrical engineering and computer science from NYU-POLY and an MS in project management from George Washington University and is the mother of two daughters, Priya and Nisha. She lives in the San Francisco Bay Area.

Karen Bairley Kruger, MS – Mother, Entrepreneur, and Social Impact Investor

Karen Bairley Kruger is an impact investor, writer, and mother of four. She holds a BA in psychology from the College of William and Mary and an MS in counseling, Phi Beta Kappa, from San Francisco State University. Karen worked previously with children and adolescents, teaching and counseling in Japan and Hawaii, respectively. She is passionate about increasing cultural awareness as a part of early education and expanding leadership opportunities for women and minorities. Karen is an active angel investor in female-founded social-impact companies. She is dedicated to leveling the playing field by empowering women to support, hire, and invest in each other.

Christine Emilie Lim, MBA - Technology Marketer

Christine Emilie Lim has extensive marketing experience in Silicon Valley both at a Fortune 500 company (Symantec) and at VC-backed technology start-ups such as Mercantila (acquired), MarketTools (acquired), Egnyte, and HackerOne. She concentrates on social enterprise investments and runs a foodtech blog on gastronomypix.com. Christine received an MBA from the Rotterdam School of Management, Erasmus University in the Netherlands and a BS in business administration in marketing and international studies from the Kelley School of Business, Indiana University, Bloomington. She has lived in multiple countries but calls Cebu City, Philippines her first home. Christine is passionate about food systems, sustainability, health, and cultures.

Wingee Sin, CAIA, CFA - Financial Products Wiz, Investor, Start-up Advisor, Traveling Skirt

Wingee is a managing director at State Street Global Advisor and heads up global product strategy for the firm's retirement business. In her capacity, she leverages her fifteen years of investment, strategy, and execution experience to drive product innovation and evolution to help America retire with dignity. She has extensive experience across global capital markets and investors. Wingee has been a serial intrapreneur in her career and had the privilege of making a difference at Goldman Sachs, Barclays Global Investor, and State Street. She loves investing and has a passion in helping others, especially women, make their money work for them.

Hana Yang, MS – International Trailblazer and Entrepreneurial Ecosystem Builder

Hana Yang is a senior banker on First Republic Bank's tech and venture team, whose mission is to foster community and thought leadership in the entrepreneurial and venture capital ecosystem. Prior to First Republic, she was a managing partner at Manos Accelerator, an accelerator for Latino founders. She also has strategic and operational experience in crowdfunding and e-commerce start-ups. Before joining the early-stage tech industry, Hana held positions at Adobe, the United Nations Population Fund Agency, and Capgemini Consulting. Hana is also a founding partner of Wingpact, and a Class 20 Kauffman Fellow. She received her master's degree in fund-raising management from Columbia University and her undergraduate degree in Spanish and Portuguese Literature from UC Berkeley. Hana is passionate about people, cultures, revolutionary ideas, disruptive technology, and impact investing.

Contributing Authors

Geri Stengel, Founder and President, Ventureneer

Geri is founder and president of Ventureneer, a content marketing, marketing research and education company that helps companies reach small businesses. Clients include CNBC, Dell, Intuit, New York City and turnstone. As a writer (author of *Forget the Glass Ceiling: Building Your Business Without One* and *Stand Out In the Crowd: How Women (and Men) Benefit From Equity Crowdfunding* and *Forbes* contributor writing about the success factor of women entrepreneurs), consultant, teacher (Kauffman FastTrac facilitator and former adjunct professor at The New School) and speaker, Geri has helped thousands of entrepreneurs take their vision to reality, develop their business plan, and learn the strategies and tactics they need to grow their businesses.

A graduate of the corporate world, Geri conducted market research for *the Wall Street Journal,* headed marketing for Dow Jones' online services and launched Physicians' Online before the Web.

Susan Preston, Managing Member, Seattle Angel Fund

Susan Preston is the general partner for the CalCEF Clean Energy Angel Fund and the managing partner for the new Seattle Angel Fund, committed to fostering entrepreneurial growth in the Pacific Northwest through early-stage investments. She teaches in the MBA program at the University of Washington. Susan also serves as co-chair and a lead instructor for the Angel Resource Institute, a global investor and entrepreneur education organization, and is a board member for Element 8, a Seattle-based angel group focusing on clean-tech investing. As an Entrepreneur-in-Residence with the Ewing Marion Kauffman Foundation for six years, she focused on initiatives supporting the growth and success of women entrepreneurs and initiatives related to angel investing and angel organizations.

Susan consults internationally on angel and venture financing, has held several board positions with public and privately held corporations, and has served on numerous nonprofit boards. She spent much of her earlier career in senior management positions in public and private companies, was a partner in two national law firms, and is a licensed patent attorney. She received her JD, cum laude, from Seattle University School of Law and her BS, magna cum laude, Phi Beta Kappa, in microbiology and public health from Washington State University.

Table of Contents

Introduction:
Wingpact Is Born

Systemic bias and unequal access to opportunities are two of the world's most significant challenges. Yet none of us has the power to tackle these issues alone; it takes collective thought, inspiration, and action to understand and address them. We wrote this book to enlighten and inspire women and men of all backgrounds—and to demonstrate that applying financial resources can be a powerful catalyst for positive social change.

Maybe you picked up this book because you liked the title. Maybe a friend gave it to you. Or maybe you are interested in taking responsibility for your financial future. Now maybe you are wondering, "What does angel investing have to do with me?" You might be thinking, "I am not that kind of person."

We hope you'll suspend your disbelief. One thing all the women contributors to this book have in common is that, at some point in our lives, we did not think of ourselves as the kind of people who:

- take financial risk

- feel empowered to change the world

- have capital at our disposal

The six coauthors of this book met in 2013 as participants in Pipeline Angels, previously called the Pipeline Fellowship—an angel investing bootcamp for women that works to increase diversity in the US angel investing community and creates capital for women social entrepreneurs. Our like-mindedness in the areas of financial mobilization and social impact, in addition to our dynamic group cohesion, made us realize we could embark on more significant work together.

After our last Pipeline class came the question: "Now what?" As enlightening as Pipeline Angels had been, we felt the need for a resource we could carry forward as we embarked on our evaluation of companies in which we might want to invest. We came up with the idea of creating this book. Soon after, we had our first meeting at Jagruti's home. Fortified by homemade Indian food and ample chocolate, we brainstormed ideas for what we could carry forward, both in the book and in our investing future. Angels have wings; we are interested in investing for impact. The idea of impact with wings was born. And we made a pact with each other around our commitment; hence: Wingpact.

We collaborated for more than a year, poring over research and interviewing prominent experts in the fields of impact investing, social entrepreneurship, and gender and racial inequity.

Our goals in writing this book were to:

- share our experiences, discoveries, and journeys as individuals and as a group

- invite others to take a closer look at the power in their finances

- encourage readers to reflect on their deepest values

- motivate women and men to invest in companies that are making a positive difference in the world or seek funding for their own ideas

- offer practical advice and information for those new to angel investing

- reassure women considering starting a company that there are a growing number of women angel investors waiting to support them.

While the majority of this book focuses on the importance of women investing in women, we sincerely believe that all investors and all entrepreneurs—as well as *potential* investors and entrepreneurs—will benefit from the stories and statistics we share.

We chose to present our research along with stories of our personal journeys and how each of us came to be an angel investor. And we invited two accomplished women, Geri Stengel and Susan Preston, to contribute chapters in their areas of expertise. The intention is to demonstrate that anyone, regardless of background, class, ethnicity, or gender, has the power to mobilize others financially or create a business with impact. We hope every reader will find something in one of our personal stories that speaks to you.

The exciting thing about this book is that it's not written for a small, elite group of women. The stories, advice, and clear explanations set forth in these chapters are intended to help all women and men understand how investing in female-founded companies really can change the world.

—*Suzanne, Jagruti, Karen, Christine, Wingee, and Hana*

PART I:
Women and the Lay of Their Land: Investing, Funding, and Entrepreneurship

The following chapters provide an overall view of the trends that make this a great time for women to be involved in angel investing, some practical information for assessing potential investments, and an idea of how angel investing is making an impact around the world. Some of the authors interweave their own stories, helping connect the big picture with the personal.

Chapter One

What the Numbers Say: Angel Investing Is Not Just a Man's Game

By Geri Stengel

I've been part of the women's entrepreneurship scene since the late 1990s. I was on the board of the New York City chapter of the National Association of Women Business Owners for eight years. I cofounded an educational conference company in the early 2000s to help women pass the $1 million mark in revenue (which women reach at one-third the rate of men).

Three years ago, my passion to get women on the radar as leaders of mega-firms led me to start writing as a contributor to *Forbes*. I wanted to encourage aspiring women entrepreneurs to go for the brass ring by providing real-life examples of women who had done it. As they say, seeing is believing.

Women face greater challenges when raising money for the companies they launch and grow. Like it or not, the reality is that people are more likely to invest in people who are like them. As a result, men are more likely to invest in male entrepreneurs and women are more likely to invest in female entrepreneurs. While venture capitalists have been slow to understand the importance of having women as investment decision-makers, women have not been standing idly by. They are becoming angels and starting venture funds. For the last three years, I've been tracking and writing in *Forbes* about the rising number of women angels and their impact on female entrepreneurs' ability to raise equity financing.

I've advanced my message that women can and do start companies that grow into mega-firms in other ways as well. In 2014, Dell commissioned me to write *Forget the Glass Ceiling: Build Your Business Without One*. In 2015, I embarked on another research project aimed at helping women entrepreneurs get the funding they need through crowdfunding. I walked the walk and talked the talk, crowdfunding the project to experience first-hand what it's like to undertake a crowdfunding project on Plum Alley, a rewards-based crowdfunding platform for women. While what you get in exchange for your money is different in equity crowdfunding versus reward crowdfunding (shares in a company versus a tangible item or service, respectively), the marketing tactics are similar. The result: *Stand Out In the Crowd: How Women (and Men) Benefit From Equity Crowdfunding*, commissioned by Dell and Ellenoff Grossman & Schole. Both are available for free on Ventureneer.com.

A sea change is underway and the rising tide of female investors is—and will continue to be—part of the transformation. This is wonderful news on many fronts. Apart from allowing some of us to utter a long-overdue *it's about time*, the numbers I discuss in this chapter confirm that it's a great moment to be a woman in the world of entrepreneurship, whether you are starting a venture or investing in one. That means it's a great time to dive into a book like this, where you'll get a big-picture view of the world of angel investing from a woman's perspective, learn some practical details, and hear some truly inspiring stories.

For the longest time angel investing was a man's game in which few women participated. The numbers show this is changing, but we need it to change even more. If we want more women scaling companies to great heights, we need to fund these companies from the get-go. Women angel investors can make this happen.

Angel investing is risky business, so it's not something to approach casually. However, it can provide not only a financial return on investment but also a social and personal return, as many of the stories in this book reveal. This book is intended to inspire women who have the wealth and risk tolerance to take the plunge into angel investing. But, while angels are high-wealth individual investors,[1] you don't necessarily need to fit this category right now to be inspired and to begin getting involved through some of the newer and lower risk platforms, such as those described in Chapter Six, on crowdfunding.

Perhaps most importantly, by getting involved (even if only by reading and passing along this book), you'll become an important part of what is contributing to this change. There are two big reasons more women are getting involved in angel investing: because they want to give back and because they want to participate in an active, not passive, form of investing. Call it the tipping point, the snowball

---

1   According to the Securities and Exchange Commission (SEC), angels must be accredited investors, defined as those who have a net worth that is greater than $1 million (excluding a primary residence) or have earned more than $200,000 per year ($300,000 for couples) for the past two years with the expectation that the income will continue in the current year.

effect, or going viral. Quite simply, we are more likely to get into the game when the playing field looks like a place we can see ourselves.

Angels are Indispensable

Approximately 316,600 angels invested $24.1 billion in 73,400 ventures in the United States in 2014, according to the Center for Venture Research. This is about half the amount of money venture capitalists invest, which was $48 billion, according to the MoneyTree Report, a study of venture capital investment activity in the US. Angels are more likely than VCs to focus on seed- and start-up-stage companies.

Angels play an important role in launching the future major companies of the world, says Sonja Hoel Perkins, founder of Broadway Angels. Every major technology company was started with the help of angels, she continues. And angels provide much more than money. They provide introductions to major customers, key employees, and vendors as well as additional funding. They also mentor and provide strategic advice.

Women Build and Leverage the Ecosystem

Venture capitalists take note: female angels recognize the innovations of women entrepreneurs and are driving growth in an undervalued sector. It has happened in fits and starts, as evidenced by the ups and downs in the year-to-year changes in the number of women angels over the course of the past ten years. The dazzling one- and ten-year growth is something to celebrate.

As mentioned earlier, angels are high-wealth individual investors. More and more women fit this description. After all, women are making and controlling a larger percent of wealth these days, as Wingee discusses in Chapter Three. Happily, they are investing that wealth in each other, underwriting innovative products and services that rev up the economy. According to the Center for Venture Research, in 2014:

- 26% of all angels were women, an impressive 43% increase over the previous year

- 36% of all companies seeking funding were women-led, a whopping increase of 83% over the previous year

- 28% of all companies receiving funding were women-run, a substantial 44% increase

- 15% of all women-run companies succeeded in raising capital vs. 22% for their male counterparts

Now, don't let that last number make you glum. Remember, the percentage of companies led by women increased in all categories. "Typically, when there is a surge in the number of entrepreneurs seeking angel funding, the overall yield [success rate] goes down," says Jeffrey E. Sohl, director of Center for Venture Research. The 15 percent success rate is within the historic norms for entrepreneurs raising capital.

37 Angels founder Angela Lee wasn't surprised by the positive change in these numbers. She and other savvy angels have been making it happen. Lee's organization sources high-potential deals and coordinates due diligence

for angels investing in companies led by both men and women. It also trains angels and is part of the growing eco-system that supports women entrepreneurs and investors.

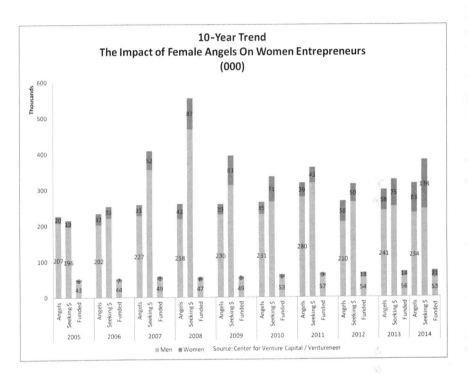

Women Angels Make Great Returns and Pay Them Forward

Springboard Enterprises and Astia were among the earliest players in the ecosystem, providing leadership training as well as access to capital for women starting in 1999. Broad-way Angels, also part of this burgeoning ecosystem, was started to show the world that women make great investors. It has certainly succeeded in that goal. While only 7 percent of the general angel-funded businesses go on to get venture capital, a whopping 70 percent of Broadway Angel companies do, says Perkins of Broadway Angels.

Superangel groups with venture funds that invest solely in women-run companies, like Golden Seeds and Belle Capital, also came into being in the last ten years. Other angel groups and venture funds do not focus solely on investing in women-run companies but, because women lead the funds, they are far more likely to invest in women. Aspect Ventures, Boldcap Ventures, and Illuminate Ventures are among the venture capital firms who recognize what women have to offer. Pipeline Angels (which brought together the authors of this book) and 37 Angels conduct formal training for aspiring women angels. Such training is critical to the growth of female angels.

One of the biggest incentives to invest in women-led companies has been the bottom line. More and more research indicates that women-run companies perform better. The ten-year trends illustrate the impact of this expanding ecosystem. Since 2005:

- the number of male angels has grown 13%, but the number of female angels has grown a whopping 318%

- the number of male entrepreneurs seeking funding grew by only 25%, while the number of female entrepreneurs seeking funding has exploded by 635%

- the number of angels backing all-male teams has grown 22%, and the number of women-owned angel-backed companies has jumped an impressive 234%

Marketplace Trends Bode Well for an Increasing Number of Women Angel Investors

Women control and create the fastest-growing segment of the world's wealth. They control 39 percent of investable assets in the US, according to *Harness the Power of the Purse: Winning Women Investors*, by Andrea Turner Moffitt. "Women want to use their financial muscle to advance women," she says.

Anecdotal evidence from Turner Moffitt's research suggests women have a deepening interest in investing in women entrepreneurs because of the personal connection they feel. Angel investing is personal and a way to pay it forward by using your expertise to influence the trajectories of other women-run companies.

As women control a greater percentage of wealth—and because they are typically less self-assured about investing it than men—angel groups increasingly attract women to investment by offering training, says Susan Preston of the Angel Resource Institute and Seattle Angel Fund. Preston, who contributed the chapter on due diligence to this book, is spearheading a new initiative called Women First Enterprises focused on educating and training women entrepreneurs and angel investors around the world. Another initiative to watch is the Learn-By-Doing Angel Funds from Portfolia, a crowdfunding platform, which allows novice women investors to train alongside highly experienced angels to build a diversified portfolio of investments via Portfolia.

Become a Risk-Astute Angel Investor

"Angel investing is not for the risk averse," as Natalia Oberti Noguera, founder and CEO of Pipeline Angels, likes to say; "it is for the *risk astute*." To determine if angel investing is for you, Preston suggests you ask yourself a series of questions. She knows the questions to ask because she trains people to become angels through Pipeline, Angel Capital Association, and her own initiative.

The first questions to ask are financial:

- Do you have the income or have the assets to be an angel investor?

- Can you afford to lose your investment without impacting your lifestyle?

- Do you have money to do multiple deals? Success in angel investing is based on the law of averages. No single investment is a guaranteed winner, but by investing in a portfolio of a minimum of 10 companies or, ideally, 20 companies, the odds are that you'll succeed. It takes an average of five to eight years to get a return on your investment.

The second set of questions relate to commitment:

- Do you have the 40 to 50 hours and sometimes 80 to 100 hours per company needed for the due diligence?

Even if you share the analysis work with other angels, you still must spend time evaluating every potential investment. Statistics have shown that the more time you spend on analysis, the more likely you are to get a good return on your investment.

- Are you willing to give more than money to the company in which you invest? It may be that your expertise and connections are even more valuable for the up-and-coming entrepreneur. This is an important additional value angels can add.

Lastly, ask yourself about your motivation:

- Do you want a return on investment? If you don't, make a donation to a nonprofit instead.

- Do you want to be useful in a variety of ways? Mentoring, advising, and connecting entrepreneurs can accelerate the target company's development and be very rewarding to the investor.

- Do you want to give back to the community? Angels play an important role in funding high potential start-up companies.

- Do you like the entrepreneur and want to see her succeed?

"Invest no more than 10 percent of your portfolio in private companies and don't do it all at one time," says Preston. "Invest over a period of time. Know that some of your companies will strike out, some will be singles, doubles, and even triples. A rare few will be home runs."

Finding a Way In

If you are just getting started in angel investing, crowdfunding platforms such as AngelList, CircleUp, Crowdfunder, and Portfolia offer an easy entry point. Many curate and vet deals. You can invest alongside more experienced investors in what are called syndicates. Investment minimums are frequently lower than they would be if you invested offline. Read more in this book's chapter on crowdfunding or even more in *Stand Out In the Crowd: How Women (and Men) Benefit From Equity Crowdfunding*, available for free on Ventureneer.com.

The Big "Why"

The motivations of women angels often go beyond simply making money. In this book, you'll hear from women who see angel investing as a form of empowerment, as a powerful tool for bolstering emerging economies, and a catalyst for personal and social change.

Gender-diverse angels are showing the impact that they have on gender-diverse entrepreneurs. Women don't need to become more like men or to follow the established rules. We have the money, the smarts, and the wealth to build high-growth, innovative businesses—and make our own rules as part of a new entrepreneurial ecosystem.

Chapter Two

Setting the Stage and Unpacking the Trends

by Suzanne Andrews

Setting the Stage:
How I Came to Write This

"I want to have a place at the table where the future is created."

These words popped into my head seemingly from nowhere. They shocked me because, for years prior to that moment, I had not cared much what, if anything, I did with my life. I was in the midst of surviving a life crisis: my twenty-year marriage had fallen apart and with it my plans to raise my two precious children in an intact, healthy family. The distress of these events had me carrying the image in my head of a small boat in a stormy Winslow Homer painting, completely out of control and in danger of sinking.

Even on my darkest, wettest days, I knew I wanted to be there for my children. Raising my son and daughter to blossom into their true amazing selves has always been my most important work and I wanted to finish it. Still, I had no personal aspirations remaining after what I felt to be the devastation of my dearest dreams.

Then something unexpected occurred, something I knew happened to other women but never thought would happen to me. I learned, during the course of the divorce activity, that I would need to get a job—after thirteen years as a full-time mother.

I had been a software engineer before I became a mother. I knew I no longer had the passion for software engineering that I would need if I wanted to update my skills and reenter the field. Luck intervened and, within a few weeks, a long-time friend hired me to work at the Anita Borg Institute (ABI), an organization dedicated to advancing women in technical careers. My friend needed me to help administer the TechWomen program. TechWomen is a program of the US State Department, founded under Hillary Clinton, that brings technical women leaders from the Middle East and North Africa to participate in mentorships with women technologists in Silicon Valley. I was pleased that my technical background had led me to a job that had meaningful social impact.

Those unexpected words about creating the future leaped into my head as I drove home from an orientation meeting connecting TechWomen's forty or so newly arrived Emerging Leaders (as they were called) with their sixty-plus mentors. The meeting had been held in a large conference hall at a prominent Silicon Valley company, with the women gathered at round tables for eight. We had played ice-breaking games and heard speeches from dynamic women technology executives.

Where had those words about creating the future come from? I had never had such aspirations, even before my current life crisis. I believe the genesis of those words had something to do with the powerful and irresistible energy I felt in the room with those TechWomen. These were women from around the globe, all pushing progress in their respective communities, many working against challenges I had never come close to personally encountering. They were optimistic, determined, adventurous, and warm. My theory is that magic happens when we are surrounded by high-achieving visionary women. That magic had made me one of them. I was going to join them in creating the future.

That magic brought me here and explains why I am writing this book.

I encountered a lot of new ideas while working on the TechWomen program at ABI. For example, I learned that women entrepreneurs are statistically more successful than men, yet remain underfinanced. This sounded like an opportunity to me and I resolved to learn what it would take to invest in women-run companies. But more than an opportunity, it seemed like a next step toward my newly articulated yearning to have a place at the table where the future is created. It might be a way to make positive social change while earning the money I needed to support myself and my children, including paying their college tuition!

I soon left ABI, became an angel investor, and learned what a powerful tool women's financial resources can be. This has been my ongoing journey out of the swirling waters of a major life pivot, the rediscovery and remaking of Suzanne.

I feel so grateful to be surrounded by a new circle of women, called Wingpact. My cofounders are ambitious big thinkers, and they inspire me to undertake (and sometimes drag me into) bigger work than I would ever imagine for myself. They also love me.

That love is where the magic—and the unstoppable power—of a circle of women originates.

The Women's Entrepreneurial Ecosystem

There has never been a better time to participate in angel investing as a woman. New structures and supports for women launching their own businesses are being developed *right now*. Anyone participating has an opportunity to help design this new economy, created by and for women, where we can thrive and work according to the values that are important to us.

Multiple trends are converging to generate an environment in which women can create a new future through business and economics. This is an exciting time for what we are calling *the women's entrepreneurial ecosystem*: the organizations, structures, and players surrounding women entrepreneurs and supporting them in their success. There is the sense that a new economy, driven by women and played out by women, is about to explode.

What Do the Trends Tell Us?

This sense of an impending explosive change for women is not just a feeling. Women entrepreneurs have been active in the United States and globally for a long time. The difference now is the growth in the number of women stepping into all the roles that surround women founders, from investors to board members and advisors. Yes, women still compose the minority and face ongoing challenges and obstacles. But our small numbers are growing; we are approaching a tipping point that will allow us to have significant impact on and control of our own futures. The women's leadership and networking organizations are mature and thriving. We have more women investors at all stages. We even have the first start-up incubators focusing on women-founded businesses.

Let's look at a few of the current trends that are making angel investing a compelling option for women.

- There are more women investors, and new initiatives to bring in even more.

- Women are increasingly stepping up to put all of their financial resources to work.

- Women are leaving the corporate world.

- New businesses are increasingly focusing on the consumer space.

More Women Investors and More on the Way

The number of women angel investors, as well as the percentage of angel investors who are women, has been increasing steadily over the past ten years. The numbers are still very low, but the small pool of experienced, intelligent, highly capable women investors is starting to gain visibility. Entrepreneurs can find them, and women interested in becoming investors have some role models and access to mentoring. (You read about some of the numbers reflecting these trends in Geri Stengel's introduction.)

One key to this growth is the new focus on education and training for women investors. The Kauffman Fellows program has been training venture capitalists since 1994. The program has intentionally focused on including women in its classes, and more than 25 percent of the participants have been women, with that number increasing recently. The Angel Resource Institute is another well-known organization that focuses on training angel investors.

We now have new education resources in this space that focus specifically on the needs of women considering angel investing. For example, Pipeline Angels launched in 2011. It began by training women in New York to become angel investors, focusing on investing in women-run social impact companies. By 2014, the organization was training women in ten cities around the country. Pipeline Angels training course is designed with women in mind.

Another organization doing the work of unleashing women's financial power is Women INVESTING in Women, founded by Ms. Anu Bhardwaj in 2011. Women INVESTING in Women is a coalition and a media platform focused on broader access to capital for companies and projects empowering women and girls. The organization holds conferences all over the world. One area of focus at these conferences is introducing women to angel investing.

Wingpact, the company founded by the authors of this book, is another new initiative created to activate new women angel investors. We hope that, after reading this book, many of you will become inspired to get involved in investing in and creating companies that you care about. Wingpact's ongoing focus includes programs to bring the idea of angel investing to qualified women who otherwise have never considered it and to create community for women investors to support them moving forward.

After steady gains for years, statistics showed the percentage of women angel investors dipping in 2013. This finding initially caused some hand-wringing and worry that the inclusion of women in the start-up ecosystem had taken a step backwards. Also, it created concern among those hoping that women investors would step up to support women entrepreneurs. But these statistics hide a more exciting reality, according to Trish Costello, CEO of Portfolia and longtime leader in the Kauffman Foundation's work to advance the cause of women entrepreneurs. Trish sees, in her wide circle of women movers and shakers, that many women who previously practiced as angels now are temporarily dropping out of angel investing to pursue bigger fish. Women are starting their own venture capital funds.

According to many studies, women actually are more successful investors than men. From this information, we can reasonably expect that the funds being launched by these experienced, gutsy women have the capacity to be some of the best-performing venture capital funds we have ever seen.

One additional benefit of more women participating in equity investing is that investors often take a seat on the board of directors of the companies they finance. Tristen Langley, founder of Amalfi Capital, intentionally uses this tradition to place women on the boards of the companies that her fund invests in. One benefit of this experience on boards is that it makes these women more valuable as angel investors and advisors to start-up companies and as mentors to other women. This feeds and continues the trends we discuss here that make now a great time to become an angel investor.

Women Ante Up

Historically, women have held less social and economic power than men. We see men all around us building large corporations and reaping the profits. We see male venture capitalists, investment bankers, stockbrokers, fund managers, and even prominent male philanthropists. It seems that men control all the money.

But is this really true? In fact, the amount of wealth that women control, as well as the rate at which their wealth is increasing, is reaching extraordinary levels.[2] According to Oppenheimer's 2006 study "Women and Investing," more than half of the investment assets in the US were already controlled by women by that time.[3] Ninety-five percent of women are directly involved in their household's financial decision-making and 25 percent are the primary

2   Ettinger, Heather R and O'Connor, Eileen M., Women of Wealth Survey (2011) Family Wealth Advisors Council. Available at: http://hemingtonwm.com/wp-content/uploads/2013/11/FWAC _WomenOfWealth.pdf

3   Quist-Newins, Mary, "Untapped Market: Women May Be Gaining Economic Power, but ..." (March 1, 2010), available at www.financial-planning.com/fp_issues/2010_3/untapped-market -2665922-1.html.

decision-makers.[4] Note that 60 percent of high net-worth women have earned their own fortunes.[5] In addition to developing their own successful careers, women tend to outlive men, and inherit their husband's and family's fortunes. These facts lead many experts in the financial planning industry to predict that women will control two-thirds of the wealth in the US by 2030.[6] While the percentages are smaller globally, women were estimated to control 27 percent of the world's wealth in 2009,[7] which is enough to create significant influence in their communities and around the world.

Yet, women don't wield their wealth in the same way men do. We keep quiet about our money, not wanting others to feel uncomfortable. Often, when we make large philanthropic gifts, we do so anonymously. Perhaps our psychology leads us to save our money and take fewer risks with it. I spoke about this with Jackie Gutierrez, founder and CEO of Hemheist, an online fashion retailer committed to ethical and sustainable manufacturing. She recalled that the businesswomen in her family would use the money they earned to support their families, often more reliably than the

---

4 Prudential Research Study, "Financial Experience and Behaviors Among Women" (2010-2011), available at http://www.prudential.com/media/managed/Womens_Study_Final.pdf

5 Stengel, Geri, "11 Reasons 2014 Will Be A Breakout Year For Women Entrepreneurs," *Forbes* (Jan. 8, 2014) available at http://www.forbes.com/sites/geristengel/2014/01/08/11-reasons-2014-will-be-a-break-out-year-for-women-entrepreneurs/

6 Ettinger, Heather R and O'Connor, Eileen M., Ibid.

7 Damisch, Peter et al, "Leveling the Playing Field" (July 2010) The Boston Consulting Group, available at: http://www.bcg.com/documents/file56704.pdf

men. Perhaps there is a psychology of motherhood, even for those of us who are not mothers. We need to save our money to make sure that our families will be safe. Maybe we feel comfortable taking risks only after the children are cared for.

There are good reasons why women handle their money differently than men do. Pressuring women to behave financially more like men is not a solution. We measure the trade-offs of risk differently. Our families and our communities benefit tremendously from our responsible and thrifty management of resources. Yet, it may also be true that we are not taking hold of the power that financial resources afford us.

What would happen if women began using our significant financial resources more effectively to create the kind of world where all people share the opportunity to pursue dreams and the potential to succeed? Women can engage in thoughtful and curious conversations and learn from each other about our ingrained belief systems, which drive our behaviors relating to money and risk. Together, we can look deeply at our financial practices and discern which are positive and which are habits that need to be challenged.

There is some evidence that we are already doing this. As women step up to offer their financial resources, they are doing so by funding projects that are important to them. In the realm of philanthropy, women are joining together in groups to evaluate charitable organizations and decide together how to best leverage their donations. The Women Donor's Network is an example of a large national group that has member-led giving circles as well as numerous strategic initiatives to support women in maximizing the impact of their collective giving. A growing number of local giving circles are springing up around the US. Melanie Hamburger, founder of Catalytic Women, has compiled and posted an impressive list of these local circles, many of which are comprised of philanthropic women who fund programs to advance women and girls.

As angel investors, too, we can put our money where our values are, as well as make a financial return. The number of women-focused angel groups is growing, reflecting the increasing number of women interested in leveraging their resources this way. The first all-women angel group in the US, Seraph Capital Forum, was founded in Seattle in 1998 by Susan Preston, one of the contributors to this book. Golden Seeds, one of the best-known women-focused early-stage investor organizations, started in 2005. We now have groups such as Astia Angels, 37 Angels, and Broadway Angels, to name just a few.

Broadway Angels is an interesting case. As an invitation-only angel group made up of world-class women investors and business executives, their investment thesis does not specify what gender entrepreneurs they invest in. They follow the best opportunities they can find in their massive deal flow. However, a quick scan of their website shows that half of their entrepreneurs are women. This example, and many others, suggests that when women bring their money to the table, opportunities for women entrepreneurs (and perhaps for entrepreneurs from other underrepresented groups) increase.

As Geri Stengel said to me in an e-mail, "Women need to ante up."

Women Step Out

For the last two or three decades at least, there has been a concerted effort on many fronts to open more opportunities to women in the corporate world. The term "glass ceiling" was invented, focusing attention on the need to move more women to upper levels of management. To help women fit in and succeed in male-dominated environments, there have been mentoring programs, dress-for-success advice, and assertiveness trainings galore. There have been many efforts to change corporate culture to be more welcoming, with diversity training, affirmative action policies, and the publication of research showing the advantages of diverse teams. There also has been a focus on bringing more women into technical careers, especially since tech companies today are having a difficult time finding enough talent. STEM programs exist at every level, serving preschool girls through moms reentering the workforce.

Women have assumed most of the burden of trying to refashion corporate life and the tech industry into places where they can feel comfortable. So much of our life energy has been poured into educating, adapting, and leaning in. We have made progress. But the gains are disappointingly small, especially considering the amount of energy expended to win them.

Increasingly, women are choosing to leave corporate careers to make their own way. When a woman starts her own business, she has much more control over her destiny. Women gain a myriad of options for ways to balance business life with family life. Women can even move beyond balance to *integration*. Work doesn't have to fit into one half of the day while mothering fits into the other half. The day can flow from one to the other as needs arise.

Also at this time, after so many years of experience in corporate life, women have gained deep expertise and skills that they can now put to use starting their own projects.

Although we have not exactly leveled the playing field, we have developed sophisticated business acumen and we know how to get things done. We can put this extensive skill set to work building our own companies and our own corporate cultures.

Women Take on the Consumer Space

Women are known to be excellent investors, especially in certain industries. Angel investors as a rule invest in companies they understand—companies they believe will generate a lot of revenue. Women are active consumers. In fact, the statistic that women are the decision-makers in 80 percent of consumer purchases is widely cited. There are whole industries that women, in general, understand better than men.

Currently, a lot of start-up companies focus on the consumer space. Historically, in Silicon Valley at least, the huge majority of start-ups seeking equity funding were in technology, an industry where many men are comfortable investing. However, women tend to have the advantage when it comes to consumer-facing companies in terms of understanding a product and knowing whether or not there will be demand for a given product. Consumer-focused founders will find that women investors get it, having a seemingly intuitive understanding of their products. This intuition is based on a lifetime of running households and families and knowing what is useful and what is not. Women have accumulated a hard-earned understanding of things like child-safety products, solutions for moms (e.g., new breast pump technology), toys and clothes for children, educational products, and many others.

This trend toward more new businesses in the consumer space will favor women angel investors. Women will be able to evaluate these businesses and make better investment decisions. This is an opportunity where women investors have an advantage and likely will see greater returns than their male counterparts.

The Opportunity: Women's Ecosystem 2.0

In the 1990s, the prevailing wisdom was that there weren't many successful women-run companies because women weren't really interested in business and money. Mainstream research supported this attitude and often was cited to explain away any perceived obstacles women faced in their business success. However, many women entrepreneurs and researchers knew these beliefs and attitudes were just plain wrong. Organizations and projects were organically and simultaneously bubbling up all over the country to support and advance women entrepreneurs.

In 1998, Trish Costello, director of Kauffman Fellows at the time, convened the Kauffman Women's Initiative and gathered fifty women leaders and thinkers from these nascent organizations. To really make change required bringing these groups together to coordinate activities and funding them adequately. This collaborative group of women made a road map, divided up tasks so they weren't duplicating each other's work, and hatched a plan to put women entrepreneurs on equal footing with men within a decade.

Many diverse organizations participated in this initiative. One was the Diana Project, a research organization that investigates equity funding trends for high-growth women-owned businesses. The purpose of the Diana project was to find and support researchers who would counter the prevailing wisdom and offer a new narrative around women entrepreneurs and their obstacles and successes. When the project began in 1999, it identified five relevant researchers. This network has now grown to more than four hundred scientists publishing work about women and entrepreneurship.

The women's ecosystem plan included identifying, expanding, and replicating model programs. All of the major economic centers around the country were targeted to create support organizations for women entrepreneurs. Springboard Enterprises, for example, was founded to support women in making connections to funding and has funneled more than six billion dollars to women entrepreneurs since its founding. The Forum for Women Entrepreneurs began around the same time and still exists as the women's leadership organization known as Watermark. The Kauffman Foundation trained angel investors, actively including women, and in 2006 created the precursor to the Angel Resource Institute to continue this function. Slowly, the percentage of women early-stage investors began to grow.[8]

All this work has led to incredible progress in women's opportunities in entrepreneurship. Yet our opportunities still don't equal men's after more than a decade. Women still face gender-based obstacles in fund-raising for their start-ups. I talked about this with Maryanna Quigless, CEO and founder of TiltFit, a fitness software company. Maryanna

---

8   From conversations with Trish Costello, June 19, 2014 and June 5, 2015.

and a number of her 2013 Stanford Graduate School of Business classmates launched start-ups upon graduation. All of her classmates had a similar level of passion and qualifications as CEOs. While a large number of the male teams were able to promptly raise more than one million dollars for their companies, Quigless didn't know of any women who had yet succeeded in securing this level of funding by the time of our conversation in June 2015. Many factors could explain this, but, as Maryanna commented to me, "Clearly, there is something going on."

Part of what may be going on is that all the data in the world does not necessarily change people's decision-making habits. In the end, investment decisions have a large emotional component. Neuroscience teaches us that people are more comfortable with people like themselves. The human brain is wired in such a way that it is very difficult for members of a dominant group to see incidents of oppression of others, even when those incidents are explicitly pointed out. It is widely accepted that the process of investment decision-making is influenced partly by pattern matching, and women are less likely to match the perceived "fundable" pattern.

Now we are starting to think about Women's Ecosystem 2.0. This new phase is less about helping women obtain access to the mainline capital sources and more about women creating their own economy. As Trish Costello so powerfully wrote to me, "After twenty years of finding ways to integrate women into the prevailing entrepreneurial and financing systems, I think the answer today is assisting women in unleashing their wealth and power in building the teams, products and worlds they want."[9]

---

9 Private e-mail, June 17, 2014.

We women of the world have an amazing opportunity right now. We have the resources, skills, and experience to create, from the ground up, a new business economy that works for women. As outlined earlier in this chapter, the infrastructure surrounding women entrepreneurs is solidifying and the roles in these structures are being filled by women. More and more support groups for women entrepreneurs are appearing, and many of them are more specific in their focus than the early groups, giving each woman more exactly what she needs. We have more women angels, more venture capitalists, women-oriented funds of all stripes, and investing education. We even have start-up incubators such as the Women's Startup Lab in Silicon Valley and MergeLane in Boulder, Colorado, as well as multiple women's coworking spaces in the planning stages. But there is a crucial opportunity—or pitfall, depending on how you look at it—in building this new ecosystem. *We must make sure we build it so we like the business culture we end up with.*

Creating the Culture We Want to Inhabit

We have grown up in the dominant culture, so it is easy to absorb values and adopt habits from that culture that do not necessarily serve our best interests. We have to discern which of our internalized beliefs we want to propagate and which we want to move away from.

One of the main reasons women are stepping out of the dominant corporate business culture and creating their own business ecosystem is that the dominant system does not work for us. Things are moving fast in building the future.

We could easily end up with a new parallel economy that has a lot of the traits we don't like in prevailing systems. We could build a new economy by and for women, but still be exhausted, burned out, and blocked from fully manifesting our talents. Alternatively, we could create a new business environment that incorporates the best of the existing culture and also values our contributions and gives us a chance to live healthy, balanced lives and the opportunity to create and build lots of great stuff. This is why we must be intentional and mindful of the culture we want to foster as we shift toward a new way of doing things.

This should be a global conversation. Women entrepreneurs around the globe all need the support of women investors. All women share some similar experiences, and we also have incredibly interesting differences that we can learn from. (You will read more about this in future chapters in this book.)

We have an opportunity to define the values that are important to us both in our local circles and as global women. Then, once we know our values, we can check each of our business practices and choose the ones that support our values. Where our practices don't match our important values, we can create new practices together that do. We can take the best of the existing mainline start-up business culture and marry it with our values.

Women, Psychology, and Money

One example of a place where women can work together to define values and create practices from those values is in the area of women's psychology around money. Some women's angel investing groups are regularly criticized (by both women and men) for conducting overly onerous due diligence. Angel investing is inherently risky, and these women angels are risk-averse—or so the story goes. This is seen as a problem because entrepreneurs are busy. It's in everyone's best interest that they focus on building their businesses, not on supplying unnecessary documentation to potential investors.

This criticism opens an opportunity for a powerful conversation among women investors. Many of our woman-centered values and practices are an improvement over the dominant entrepreneurial ecosystem and business culture. But, some of our ingrained modes of operating may not serve our higher purposes. Figuring out which is which is the challenge. Is more rigorous due diligence a benefit or a drawback? As women, we are the experts on our own psychology. We can tap each other's wisdom to sort out the transformational from the habitual and decide whether our practices are advantageous or not.

Denise Brosseau[10] has spent decades building women's entrepreneurial ecosystems by founding support organizations for women entrepreneurs, including Springboard, Watermark, and Invent Your Future Enterprises. She is currently CEO of the Thought Leadership Lab. Her commitment to women is unsurpassed. In discussing this dilemma, she says, "We must start with a conversation about cultural norms around women and money and risk. From there, we can determine sensible practices."

This is a place where women who get involved in angel investing can participate in building norms and best practices.

---

10   http://www.thoughtleadershiplab.com/AboutDenise

The chance to create an entrepreneurial ecosystem optimized for everyone's success is a heady opportunity. To do it, we must not shy away from challenging each other to grow. We must embrace all of our perspectives and use them to create a more inclusive and supportive business culture. More open conversations about women's psychology around money and risk are an example of how we can share our deep wisdom and create a new world.

Identifying Our Values

Given this opportunity to create our own culture, there are many values that women might want to integrate into our work lives. As we move ahead building companies and organizations, we will keep an eye on what is important to each of us individually and to all of us collectively. Already we have some ideas about values that are important to women in the workplace. For example, some of the feminine values that have been identified through research and discussions are collaboration, support, community, and humility. Let's examine these briefly so we can discuss them further as they relate to practices.

Collaboration

Mainstream business culture places a greater emphasis on competitiveness and fairness than many women naturally would. We look to collaboration for a broader definition of winning, and much of our innovation and creativity springs from this place.

Support

Women particularly enjoy and thrive in a supportive environment. We benefit from encouragement and find it satisfying to provide encouragement to others. We bring out the best in one another more effectively through a supportive culture than in a competitive environment. We challenge each other to grow through valuing each other's experience and wisdom, and looking after each other's well-being.

Community

Healthy community is important to women. We like to be among friends and colleagues who know one another well and uphold a culture of respect. The value we place on healthy community leads us to prioritize inclusivity and sustainability. We derive satisfaction from contributing positively to our community and making life better for others.

Humility

Women may decide to incorporate honesty about our own capabilities into the business environment. Women may prefer humility over a typical business style that sometimes feels like bravado. Perhaps we find integrity in being straightforward and humble.

This thinking around creating new business practices and culture centered around women-friendly values is in its infancy. As women share their thinking and continue to collaborate, more insights will emerge. Some values will be held commonly held by women globally. Local groups of women can also explicitly determine the values by which they want to work.

Wingpact is an example of a circle of women consciously choosing values important to them collectively. The six Wingpact founding partners have chosen the following set of five core values to drive our work:

- *Influence*: we influence the global community by supporting women.

- *Inspire*: we inspire each other and all women to manifest their greatest good.

- *Innovate*: we create and support innovation that disrupts the gender-biased status quo.

- *Invest*: we invest to make a difference long-term.

- *Impact*: we seek impact that creates equal opportunity for all.

These are the deep passions we at Wingpact have found in our hearts and that are expressed through the writing of this book and all Wingpact activities. Whatever values women choose to express in our newly emerging business ecosystem, the important thing is that we consciously choose what is important to us and intentionally match our practices to our values.

The opportunity to create and share new business practices that support women's values is boundless. You can participate in this exciting area of new knowledge creation as a woman angel investor. The next section examines practices developed around investing that reflect some of the values discussed above. These are examples of innovative practices we can develop when we consider what is collectively important to us in our work life.

Defining Practices for the Women's Entrepreneurial Ecosystem

Building our own entrepreneurial ecosystem presents us with innumerable opportunities to develop new ways of doing things that suit women's work styles. Women CEOs can run their companies according to their own values. For example, they can implement innovative employee policies and build out-of-the box partnerships, which give their companies the edge in attracting talent and making things happen. Start-up incubators and shared workspaces allow the kinds of mutually supportive relationships that women crave. Every aspect of the ecosystem can be crafted to support a new vision of a business world that adapts to women's ways of working.

This section will focus specifically on innovative practices that involve angel investors. Women are innovating ways of working together in many areas of the seed-stage investment process. Some of these are:

- teaching and learning the investment process

- women-focused angel groups

- the fund-raising process

- ongoing angel-entrepreneur relationships

Teaching and learning the investment process

As a part of the current explosion of our ecosystem, women have more options for learning the ins and outs of angel investing. Many of these options are designed specifically to meet the needs and desires of women learners.

One prominent resource is the previously mentioned Pipeline Angels. This organization was developed from the ground up with the needs of women in mind. In general, women enjoy learning new things in community, with opportunities to practice new skills in a supportive environment. Over the course of four to six months, participants receive qualitative information about aspects of angel investing that they need to know, such as evaluating companies, conducting due diligence, and structuring deals. In addition, class time includes opportunities to meet and have informal small-group conversations with experienced mentors. The final component of the class is the built-in experience of actually making an investment.

Women tend to enjoy and benefit from a number of interesting aspects of this group process.

First, learning collaboratively with a group of women is an optimal environment for many new women investors. Currently, angel investing is very male-dominated, as is the whole entrepreneurial ecosystem. Many women experience a feeling of safety and supportiveness when they have the rare opportunity to relax in an all-women group. In addition, a group of classmates can form the basis of an investing network moving forward. This network of support is essential when navigating nontraditional roles and working to make change. We women can affirm the importance of each other's dreams, even if the mainstream culture doesn't see our work as sensible.

Secondly, access to mentors is powerful for women. Pipeline Angels mentors are either women or members of other groups underrepresented in angel investing and in mainstream business in general. Connecting with successful women role models boosts the participants' confidence and motivation to push through challenges. Seeing role models of diverse backgrounds helps one envision oneself entering a business area that appears homogeneous. An additional benefit is that these mentors become part of the participants' own networks, helping bring credibility and opportunities to the new investors.

A third unique aspect of the Pipeline Angels program is the practice component, in which an investment is made together. Each class participant makes a commitment ahead of time to commit a small investment to a company chosen by the group. The participants work together to review applications, question entrepreneurs at the pitch session, narrow down the front-runners, conduct due diligence, and make a final investment decision.

A final note of interest about the Pipeline Angels training ground is its focus on social impact companies. Women are increasingly interested in doing work that has personal meaning for them. The trend of social impact for-profit business is very attractive to women, although it is a new concept for many. The social impact component of this class is an additional unique aspect that suits women especially.

Pipeline Angels is a great example of rethinking angel investor training to meet the needs of women. This training addresses the previously discussed values of collaboration, support, and community, as well as other values important to many women.

Other organizations are doing similar work in the space of training women and other underrepresented groups to become angel investors. 37 Angels is an organization that takes a number of the aspects of Pipeline Angels and reworks the format to accommodate women who prefer a different kind of schedule. Similarly, Manos Accelerator, a start-up accelerator for Latina/o entrepreneurs, trains investors who might be inclined to invest in Latina/o run companies. Hana Yang (one of the authors of this book), was a managing partner at Manos Accelerator and has launched the Manos Angel Network and created their flagship Manos Angel Bootcamp program.

Another kind of resource for women learning about angel investing is Portfolia, a platform launched by CEO Trish Costello to connect entrepreneurs and investors. Portfolia differs from other such platforms in that it has a social media aspect and allows members to follow companies and other investors over time. Additionally, Trish partners with foundations and corporations to offer funds that angels can invest in, as well as a new concept she calls "Learn-By-Doing Funds" that offer mentoring to the fund investors. It is exciting to see the creative thinking going into ways to support new investors who might want to "dip a toe in" before making huge commitments. While this platform is open to anyone and will appeal to a broad range of investors, its innovative design will support more women in feeling comfortable with equity investing.

These organizations are all doing creative thinking around how we can modify existing systems or create completely new resources to encourage all people to participate fully in supporting the projects they care about to create a future that they envision.

Women-focused Angel Groups

Another growing segment is angel investing organizations focused on women. There are many variations of these groups. Some are made up of only women investors, but invest in any entrepreneur, regardless of gender. Perhaps they focus on a certain industry or other common area of interest. Other well-known groups do not limit who their investors are, but invest only in women entrepreneurs. The groups vary in size, formality, and resources. Some are national organizations with multiple chapters around the country. Other angel groups are small, informal groups of friends who meet in each other's living rooms. Some are offshoots of longstanding support organizations for women entrepreneurs that are just now starting angel groups.

In any case, the growing presence of these women-focused groups is an exciting development for everyone involved. Now we can have women on both sides of the negotiating table. This gives us the opportunity to mold the fund-raising process to be supportive and inclusive.

Highlight on an Advantage of Women-focused Angel Groups: Pitching

Here is an example of a change to the standard fund-raising process that women involved might generally enjoy.

A typical investment pitch session might unfold as follows: the executive team of the company that is pitching to an angel group enters the room with the investors while the other teams pitching that day wait their turns outside the room. This approach presumes that the different companies are in competition and should not see each other's pitches out of fairness. In contrast, in our Pipeline Angels pitch session, all the presenting teams stayed in the room and heard each other's pitches, as well as the questions the investors asked. Seven women-run social-impact companies presented to eight investors. The entrepreneurs did leave after all the pitches were complete, giving investors a chance to discuss our observations privately.

At the time, I was fascinated by how such a simple change affected the environment. The entrepreneurs were tweeting in support of each other's companies and buying each other's products online! There was a general feeling of mutual support for—and interest in—each other's success. The entrepreneurs were, in fact, competing, since we investors had stated that we would choose one company to fund as a group. On the other hand, a few members of our group invested individually in some of the companies that pitched but were not chosen as the group finalist.

Perhaps being in competition is a matter of perspective. Seeing other companies pitch and hearing investors' questions can be a valuable learning opportunity. While this might have given an advantage to companies that pitched later in the day, this was not the perspective that prevailed at the meeting. Inviting all the entrepreneurs to stay in the room seems like a small detail in the management of the fund-raising process, but I believe it significantly changed the culture. It moved us from a winner-take-all atmosphere of competition toward collaboration, support, community, and a broader definition of winning. If we could extend this cultural shift to our whole business ecosystem, practice by practice, perhaps women (and everyone) would be more successful.

Innovating Around the Fund-Raising Process

There are many variations to the standard process of investing in early stage companies, as well as many established conventions. Here are some areas ripe for innovation, now that we can have women on both sides of the table.

Basic Respect

When women entrepreneurs talk about the value of having access to women investors, they sometimes simply comment, "I am just glad you won't try to sleep with me." We've all had such experiences or at least heard stories about them. They range from the blatant expectation of sex for funding to that hard-to-put-your-finger-on-it feeling that if you were a man, they wouldn't be talking to you like this. This seems so fundamental that it's almost shocking. Yet we can't underestimate the impact of simply treating entrepreneurs with basic respect.

These sexist experiences sap our life energy—energy we women would rather direct towards building our dreams. This is one important reason why it is so powerful to have women angel investors. Just imagine if no woman had to waste her energy asserting her right to be at the table and could instead focus completely on creating a new future.

As a woman investor, merely showing up is innovative, creative, and disruptive. Just by being ourselves, we allow entrepreneurs to assume they will be considered for the strength of their ideas and the evidence of their talents. Our presence in this area of business can unleash the full power of women's dreams.

Aggression of Numbers

Another interesting aspect of the fund-raising process is how entrepreneurs present their business to potential investors. When they pitch, entrepreneurs are expected to portray a high level of confidence in their businesses. This often translates into a certain amount of swagger and bravado. Perhaps the entrepreneur is overly optimistic about how much funding has been committed, or drops names, or creates pressure around how quickly a round will fill. Interestingly, this creative exaggeration doesn't seem to present a problem for those participating in the communications. Participants in the mainline fund-raising space apparently expect a certain amount of fluffing up of the facts, which is interpreted as confidence and seems to be integral to the success of convincing investors to invest.

Relying on stereotypes, it seems likely that a male-dominated fund-raising culture would exhibit these backslapping behaviors and bluster. Such behaviors are neither good nor bad, as long as everyone playing the game understands the rules. But many women may not be aware of these unwritten rules. Even when we become aware, we may not feel comfortable playing the game by engaging in behaviors that are foreign to us. In fact, some women may be uncomfortable enough that they feel dishonest if they follow these norms.

If a woman entrepreneur is perfectly straightforward about how much she has raised, from whom, and when, does this put her at a disadvantage? Do investors habitually deflate an entrepreneur's claims in their minds to account for the expected minor exaggerations? If so, they would see this woman's level of success as less than it actually is.

I spoke to Rachel Cook, CEO of Seeds, about this phenomenon, which she has aptly named "aggression of numbers." She says aggression of numbers creates a strange, gray area for her, where she experiences some confusion about how to present her business that her male founder friends don't necessarily feel.

She goes on to explain, "It's as though the aggression of numbers phenomenon, and my experience hearing what my male founder friends would do in situations with investors, made me feel as though I was at more of a disadvantage in just plainly and clearly stating where we were as a company. It would make me question, strategically, whether or not it was in the company's best interest for me to be fully transparent, even though that was what my instincts were telling me to do.

"And that is a huge bummer. So the only solution seems to be greater transparency all around, and the creation of a system of behavior that encourages that. I think the best investors really get this… investors tend to find it very refreshing to hear about the real, unsugarcoated problems we are facing. It increases my credibility as a founder and it invites more help when troubleshooting a problem so that we can move past challenges more quickly and effectively. So transparency really is ultimately a win-win."

We have an opportunity to decide: do we want to adopt the tactics of slight exaggeration and bravado in our pitching and fund-raising? If so, investors need to account for that in evaluating companies. Or do we want to adopt a communication style more comfortable for most women, in which we are direct about our numbers?

A corollary to this is women's documented tendency to underestimate and underplay their successes. Again, we have an opportunity to decide how we want this new woman-friendly ecosystem culture to work and to bring these unwritten rules to the surface so potential investors can take them into account. Do we encourage each other to take full responsibility for our accomplishments? Or do we encourage a culture of humility in which we downplay our accomplishments?

Supportive of Values

Women are increasingly drawn to work that is personally meaningful and that makes a positive social impact. Having access to women investors may be a great option for women entrepreneurs building social impact businesses.

Jackie Gutierrez is the founder and CEO of Hemheist, an online clothing retailer committed to ethical and sustainable manufacturing and business practices. When Jackie first started testing her pitch with investors, most of her contacts were men. Her initial experience was that investors felt there might be a trade-off between potential profits and the positive social impact aspects of Hemheist's business model, and they were not willing to take that risk. Jackie started to think she would need to compromise her values in the short term, then fold her positive practices back into the business once Hemheist became profitable. However, once Jackie started connecting with female angel investors, she found more support for sticking to her values for the company. In fact, many companies are able to implement their social values without compromising financial returns. "Many women, because of our socialization, take the advice of men too easily. Women need education on this phenomenon so they can make decisions that are best for themselves," Jackie observed. This story indicates that just having women investors in the ecosystem may help women entrepreneurs stay true to their own hearts, no matter who ultimately invests in a company.

Jackie reflected with me on her experience pitching to men compared to pitching to women. For her, pitching to women often feels more natural. Since Hemheist is an apparel company, women more often get what she is trying to do. It is easier to explain her model and hook women investors in. On the other hand, once men are hooked into her ideas, they tend to make faster investment decisions and invest larger amounts of capital.

These are qualitative, subjective stories and observations. Still, they support the idea that having access to women angel investors improves the fund-raising experience for women entrepreneurs. Even with the growing numbers, women angels can still be few and far between. Tiffany Roessler is president of ISPOSSIBLE IN TECH, a technology staffing firm delivering diverse teams. She recently made her first angel investment in the company HER, a community and dating app for lesbians. Considering the target market of HER, Tiffany told me she was astounded that she was one of only three women investors out of thirty-five.

Having more women investors in the ecosystem helps women entrepreneurs assume they will be treated with basic respect, can tell their stories in ways that feel more honest to them, and experience more support for their personal values. Even when men ultimately become the investors in a company, the presence of diverse investors seems to improve the fund-raising experience for women entrepreneurs.

The Ongoing Angel-Entrepreneur Relationship

It will be interesting to see how we evolve the ongoing relationship between angels and their entrepreneurs as more women enter investor roles.

Traditionally, investors roll up their sleeves and dive in to help with the work that can be critical to a company's success. Investors open their networks, bring in resources, forge strategic partnerships, and help with strategic planning. Investors can serve on the board of directors and keep an eye on the goals of revenue, impact, and long-term return to investors. Ideally, entrepreneurs will have enough interest to be able to pick and choose investors and will use that opportunity to bring necessary skills and resources to the team.

Shala Burroughs is a founder of CloudPeeps, a talent community that connects freelance social media, marketing, content and community professionals with remote work opportunities. She and her cofounder, Kate Kendall, experienced a wild, successful ride with their company. Starting 2014 with some modest goals, they saw demand for CloudPeeps's services explode way beyond their expectations, leading to a successful funding round during the second half of the year.

Shala and her team made a concerted effort to bring on a diverse set of investors. They are diverse in terms of gender, race, ethnic background, global location, and experience level. Shala did this because of research that shows diverse teams perform better. She also has a personal passion for and commitment to opening opportunity to all. This is a great example of an entrepreneur choosing her investor team according to the resources she wants available to her and her company in the long term. This is also a model for how we as women can work to further our values in the world with our day-to-day actions and strategic decisions.

Because of this diverse team of investors, Shala has a great perspective on the similarities and differences between male and female investors. She told me that in her experience, there are not a lot of differences in what her various investors bring—they are all fantastic members of her team who bring incredible resources to CloudPeeps. If an entrepreneur encounters a sexist male investor, they usually get weeded out of the process well before the post-investment relationship begins.

Shala does have one observation of differences between the genders when it came to her investors. She says that her women investors tend to ask more often about her well-being and remind her to take care of herself. This is an example of a practice that brings the values of community and support into a start-up's business culture. We know that women are caretakers in many areas of their lives, and one way we support the women around us is to remind each other to allocate some of that care for ourselves. Small changes such as this add up and help create a business culture where women feel at home and can more effectively focus on the work at hand.

This is just a small sampling of practices in angel investing that are making a difference for women entrepreneurs. For Wingpact, defining our values and executing to those helps us maximize our impact on the future. Even more, we are excited to be part of an ecosystem and partnering with other organizations that reflect our core values of influence, inspiration, innovation, investing, and impact.

Now is the Time to Step Up

There are so many reasons why now is a great time to get involved in the entrepreneurial ecosystem for women as an angel investor. A number of business and demographic trends support the success of women entrepreneurs and the investors who sustain them. Women have gained experience and business savvy and are increasingly taking their talent out of the corporate world and starting their own companies. More and more women are stepping up to offer their financial resources in service of exciting and meaningful projects. Consumer industries are taking off, creating opportunity for those who understand these industries by virtue of their life experiences. And women worldwide are seeking ways to increase their impact in the world and focus on work that has meaning to them.

Yet this is only the beginning of the sweeping change these trends portend. We have women-focused angel investing groups, but there is room for many more. More women-centered businesses are receiving funding, but women entrepreneurs remain underfunded compared to their success rates. Bringing more women investors into the landscape can address both of these issues.

Building a more supportive ecosystem around women entrepreneurs has the potential to change more than the success rates of individual founders and investors. We have an opportunity to recreate business practices and thus create a professional work culture that integrates values important to women and allows women to maximize the impact of all of their talents and passions. We are starting to see some small evolution in business practices where women work together. The development of best practices for inclusion (and other women's values) has nearly infinite possibilities to create an environment that works for all kinds of people.

These changes are happening worldwide. We have the opportunity to build a global community of women using the path of business to solve the persistent world problems. There are so many unknowns about how to proceed, but the excitement and possibilities when women come to the table with all of their abilities are real. We are doing it now.

Now is the time to get involved by bringing all of your resources—financial, intellectual, professional experience, creative thinking—to the global community of women creating the future.

Chapter Three

Angel Investing as a Form of Empowerment

by Wingee Sin, CFA, CAIA

"If you're lucky enough to do well, it's your responsibility to send the elevator back down."
—Kevin Spacey

I started making a living when I was quite young. As a teenager—at an age when my peers were worrying about grades and social status—I was making ends meet. This early independence meant I always managed my money (or lack of it, when I was younger) very intentionally. It was hard-earned and it wasn't just about making a living. It was about earning money to create the kind of world I want to live in—and then spending and investing it with purpose. That was how I grew up creating impact with money.

It's not surprising that I ended up as an angel investor. Angel investing is an incredibly empowering experience that can go beyond investing purely for the bottom line. You can use your financial and intellectual resources to spur innovation, create change, or disrupt the status quo. You can empower entrepreneurs who are doing amazing things like correcting market inefficiencies, realizing dreams, or making a positive impact.

The act of funding is particularly empowering for women, whether they are the funders or the funded, because of the seldom articulated connection between money and power. Money creates power; by extension, women with money are powerful.

As a self-made woman, I have thought a lot from a philosophical perspective about what it means to *make good money*. To me, *making good money* meets three goals. The first involves making ends meet for today, that is, making enough now to meet your current day's needs. The second goal is about making ends meet for future needs. Many of us don't realize that our working years are intended to produce sufficient income to sustain us during both the working years (current days) and non- (or reduced) working years (future days). This is the valuable lesson of savings—it's actually just a transfer of income from today to tomorrow. The third goal is the focus of this chapter: investing the money with a specific purpose. You can be intentional with your money so it can begin to change the world for the better.

The women who decided to write this book have achieved these three goals. Our work together forming Wingpact represents our commitment to "send the elevator back down." We all were successful and comfortable, and could easily have simply enjoyed this time in our lives. Instead, we chose to stay up late after our kids went to sleep, squeeze in conference calls after a ten-hour work day, burn the midnight oil to write (or rewrite and rewrite) a few more words, brainstorm all day on giant poster boards about inclusive entrepreneurship ecosystem models, obsess about multiple iterations of the right look and feel for our brand identity and logo, get goggle-eyed with legal contracts and financial projections—all in hopes of inspiring a few more women to not only be successful, but to *matter*.

This chapter is about how angel investing is one of the ways of fulfilling the three goals of making good money. We work hard to earn the money that we make. It's time we make our money work hard for us also. If you are someone who has never thought of your money this way before, I hope this chapter, and this book, will prompt you to think a little differently.

Women have made great strides in terms of *making* money and *accumulating* wealth (see Chapter Two for more on this). Women's wealth is growing steadily. By 2014, American women controlled close to $12 trillion in wealth.[11] Women have joined the workforce in greater numbers and are increasingly taking the lead in managing

11 https://www.bcgperspectives.com/content/articles /financial_institutions_branding_communication_leveling_the _playing_field/

their household finances. Women live longer than men and therefore inherit more wealth than their male counterparts.

While more could certainly be accomplished in terms of income equality, the next and equally important step is moving towards equality in *investing*.

Women have always been underrepresented in society. East or West—rich or poor—we have struggled to make our voices heard through many cultures and many eras. Even today, fifty years after the beginnings of women's liberation and at the forefront of the most gender-egalitarian culture the world has seen for a long time, women still struggle to find parity.

We can see one aspect of this reflected in entrepreneurship statistics. In 2013, women-owned ventures accounted for 23 percent of the entrepreneurs who sought angel capital, but only one out of every five of these women entrepreneurs received angel investments.[12] Compared to men, women entrepreneurs tend to bootstrap further than others or seek alternative forms of financing. Why? Why do women still struggle to get funding when our market is supposedly free and equal-opportunity?

Perhaps another statistic can give us the answer: women investors represent only 19.4 percent of the angel market, and less than 10 percent of the venture capital market.[13] Simply stated: *there aren't enough women investors.* Thus, the issues women tend to care about receive

---

12 http://paulcollege.unh.edu/sites/paulcollege.unh.edu/files/2013%20Analysis%20Report%20FINAL.pdf

13 Jeffrey Sohl, "The Angel Investor Market in 2013: A Return to Seed Investing", Center for Venture Research, April 30, 2014. http://paulcollege.unh.edu/sites/paulcollege.unh.edu/files/2013%20Analysis%20Report%20FINAL.pdf

less monetary attention because there are too few women investing at the seed stage.

If just *1 percent* of the $12 trillion in wealth women controlled in 2014 were allocated to angel investing today, it would create a capital pool of $12 *billion*—close to 50 percent of all US angel investments. The issues that women care about would be better represented. Women entrepreneurs, especially those on the path to social change, would face much less resistance in making their ventures a reality.

By entering the field of angel investing, I have entered an exciting, dynamic world, where my investments are changing and creating the world I live in. As women, allocating our financial and human capital to something we believe in is one of the most powerful things we can do.

Women's Impact in Entrepreneurship and Investment

"My dream is to find individuals who take financial resources and convert them into changing the world in the most positive ways."

– Jacqueline Novogratz, founder of Acumen Fund

When women do invest, they often want to take into account a company's social impact. Many women, as I did, aim to use their capital to create the world they want to live in. In a 2013 study conducted by US Trust,[14] 65 percent of women (versus 42 percent of men) believe it is important to consider the social, political, and/or environmental

---

14   http://www.ustrust.com/publish/content/application/pdf/GWMOL/ARS7ME57.pdf

impact of the companies they invest in. Twice as many women as men say that they "consider the social responsibility of investments." The wealthier the investor, the greater the difference, with 34 percent of ultra high-net-worth (UHNW) women and only 15 percent of UHNW men considering social responsibility as a factor when investing. Among millionaires, 45 percent of women and 23 percent of men say they care about the social ramifications of an investment. The trend is clear: high-net-worth women care about impact of their investments.

On the other side of the table are women entrepreneurs championing social change within their communities. According to Leigh Fiske, VP of Impact and Partnership at the Unreasonable Institute, 52 percent of the organization's ventures have had at least one female cofounder. Over the years, that percentage has been as high as 83 percent and as low as 36 percent, but the average is 52 percent between 2010 and 2014.[15]

Another example of organizations championing social change is Village Capital[16] (VilCap), which finds, trains, and funds entrepreneurs solving global problems. Their programs have supported more than 450 entrepreneurs, and VilCap-affiliated investment vehicles have invested in 51 companies through their unique peer-selection process to date. Victoria Fram, managing director at VilCap Investments (Village Capital's affiliated for-profit investment fund) noted that in research VilCap has done with Goizueta Business School at Emory University, women-run businesses are 40 percent more profitable

15   Interview with Leigh Fiske.

16   Interview with Victoria Fram.

than businesses run by men in similar sectors and regions, although they raise only 60 percent as much funding. Some additional facts:

- Twenty-five percent of Village Capital's participants are women cofounders (the average start-up accelerator is 8 percent).

- Thirty-five percent of the Village Capital investees are women.

- Women entrepreneurs participating with Village Capital cite two important characteristics of the program: 1) The investment committee of peers is far more gender-diverse than the average investment committee they usually pitch; and 2) the peer selection process rewards collaboration and transparency, two traits women entrepreneurs value.

While these are just two examples of women being involved in social entrepreneurship, they showcase opportunities to create impact—and particularly empowerment for women—with your angel investments.

More Women Means Better Performance

Multiple studies have noted that companies with a more balanced representation of female leadership tend to perform better. Catalyst's 2011 research found a 26 percent difference in return on invested capital (ROIC) between the top-quartile companies (with 19 to 44 percent female board representation) and bottom quartile companies (with zero female directors).[17] Meanwhile, McKinsey demonstrated[18] that companies with a higher proportion of women at the board level typically exhibited a higher degree of organization, above-average margins, and higher valuations.

Perhaps Yunfang Juan, a notable woman angel investor, summarizes this point best: "It has been more common for me to come across a woman entrepreneur that under-promises and over-delivers."[19]

Creating Impact as an Angel Investor

Empowerment takes forms other than money. Angel investors, unlike other types of investors, typically become board members or access points for entrepreneurs and actively advise and coach entrepreneurs in the development of their ideas. We contribute our brains (human capital) as well as our money (financial capital). As Ann Winblad, cofounder and managing director of Hummer Winblad Venture Partners, noted, "Financial capital is worth nothing if it is not coupled with great intellectual capital."[20] As an angel investor, I occupy a front-and-center role in the development of the companies I fund. I have found the impact aspect of angel investing to be incredibly empowering.

---

17   http://www.catalyst.org/knowledge/bottom-line-corporate -performance-and-womens-representation-boards-20042008

18   http://www.mckinsey.com/client_service/organization/latest _thinking/unlocking_the_full_potential

19   Interview with Yunfang Juan.

20   Interview with Ann Winblad.

The story of Prerna Gupta, a woman entrepreneur, exemplifies the ripple effect of successful angel investment. Prerna cofounded Khush, a company that developed intelligent music apps and was sold to Smule in 2011. A seed angel fund called 500 Startups invested in and mentored Prerna's company during its seed stage.

"500 Startups helped me with my company in reaching a successful exit," Prerna says, "and I want to do the same for the next generation of entrepreneurs." Prerna has since invested in the 500 Startups fund and syndicate, and is also a mentor to 500 Startups.[21]

I find the blurring of lines between investor/entrepreneur and financial backer/intellectual leader to be one of the most meaningful features of angel investment. There is a real pay-it-forward culture at work here, and I believe it is one of the keys to innovation. This makes angel investing unique, and also makes for a much larger commitment than regular investment.

My own experience moving from philanthropy to angel investing illustrates this. I had served on the board of Foundation for Sustainable Development, a nonprofit providing mission-based grants to grassroots nonprofit organizations all over the world. The work was satisfying, the organization ran well, and we made impact through projects funded with $500 to $5,000. But the impact ended there. Having been an investor for 15 years—and someone who tries every year to learn about something new to invest in—I began thinking about how investing might help with amplifying impact and sustaining the pool of capital. Philanthropists already have decided to give away their money to a cause, usually without anything in return but the satisfaction of

---

21   Interview with Prerna Gupta.

knowing they have made a difference. If that same money went toward *investing*, its impact could grow far beyond the initial project. Of course, not everyone will feel comfortable making this shift, but for me it was a new way of defining how to create and sustain social impact. I truly believe investing creates and sustains impact. I encourage you to think deeply about the change *you* would like to create in forming your investment thesis.

How Angel Investing Fits in My Portfolio

I plan to build my angel portfolios over the next decade, targeting ten to fifteen investments. The total angel portfolio size will be less than 5 percent of my investible assets. (Of course, your goals may be quite different; please consult your individual financial planner or advisor to determine what might be the appropriate allocations for your portfolio.) In creating the portfolio, there are three things that I will keep in mind:

1. I am likely going to be kissing many frogs before I find my prince. (Angel investing has a high failure rate, and most of my return might come from a single investment.)

2. This is money that I am willing to bid farewell to for a decade. (Angel investment is highly illiquid.)

3. I am thoughtful about how these investments relate to other parts of my investment portfolio. (Diversification is important.)

Let's look at each of these in more detail.

Angel Investments Have a High Failure Rate

Data from the Bureau's Center for Economic Studies[22] shows that the survival rate of angel-funded start-ups has barely hovered above or dipped below 50 percent since 1989. In any individual investment, an angel investor is more likely than not to lose money.

This means that the standards of due diligence for angel investment must be at least as rigorous as any other type of investment. As other experienced angels note, it's not uncommon to go through a hundred pitches and find only two investments appropriate for due diligence. Given the high failure rate, one of your frogs must really turn out to be a prince in order for your overall investment portfolio to deliver worthwhile risk-adjusted returns. I make every investment with the care that I would put in if it were my one and only.

Diversification does pay off: according to a study conducted by Professor Robert Wiltbank at Willamette University, the median return for investors with a portfolio of at least six investments exceeds 1X.[23] ("X" in private equity/venture capital terminology refers to the return or exit multiple for an investment. A return of 2X, for example, means a doubling of an initial investment; 1X means the investor recouped the original money invested.) But be wary of lowering your standards to build your portfolio quickly. For more detailed information about due diligence and valuation best practices, see Chapter Four by Susan Preston, head of the Woman First Enterprise and world-renowned expert in entrepreneurship and angel investing.

---

22   http://money.usnews.com/money/personal-finance/mutual -funds/articles/2013/11/27/a-guide-to-angel-investing

23   http://sites.kauffman.org/pdf/angel_groups_111207.pdf

Angel Investments Are Illiquid

It is very important to note that angel investments are private investments. They are highly illiquid and generally long-term investments. Conservatively, expect to hold them for a decade! According to Professor Wiltbank's study, the level of positive returns typically increases with length of investment; higher-return investments average longer investment periods. Among the study's investment results, exits of 1X to 5X times averaged 3.3 years, while exits of 30X times averaged six years. Furthermore, it was not uncommon to see an investment period of more than ten years. Professor Wiltbank describes this situation as "lemons ripen faster than plums."

The long-term, relatively inflexible nature of my angel investments means that I will not have access to my money for unexpected spending needs and will be unable to change allocations and rebalance if the market environment changes. Ann Winblad, cofounder of leading venture capital firm Hummer Winblad, describes angel investment capital as "capital you never need." In the worst case, I am willing to lose the money I set aside for angel investment.

Diversification and Portfolio Fit

Finally, you need to think about diversification and how your angel investments relate to other parts of your portfolio. For example, if I have a portfolio of technology start-ups, the success of my portfolio companies will likely be related to the performance of technology stocks or real estate value in Silicon Valley. Put another way: if I have significant company stock in a particular industry segment, and my angel investments are *also* concentrated in the same industry (which happens quite often, as people's domains of expertise are typically not uniformly diverse), my overall exposure to this industry segment will be extremely high. From a risk management perspective, I need to be careful of putting too many eggs in one basket.

On the other hand, your knowledge in the public sector potentially can inform your choices in the private sector. As an example, I have a keen interest in the credit card segment of the financial services industry (I think someday we will bid farewell to cash), and have long followed Visa, MasterCard, and American Express as public companies. My knowledge of these three companies helped when I was considering the financial technology payment start-ups that are currently disrupting the segment. My investment knowledge from one part of my portfolio contributed to another, and vice versa.

While everyone's circumstances are different, typical angel investors are aware of these caveats. They allocate a small proportion of their overall investment portfolio to angel investments (usually less than five or ten percent) and consult a financial advisor to see what allocation might be appropriate for their circumstances. I cannot reiterate enough how important it is to keep the time frame of investment in mind. Above all, you need to be comfortable not seeing your capital for quite a while.

Different Ways to Become an Angel Investor

There are four main ways you can become an angel investor:

1. Invest independently, as a direct angel

2. Invest via an angel or seed fund

3. Participate in a syndicate

4. Join an angel investing network

Direct Angel Investing

Investing *directly* means that you exchange financial and human capital for convertible debt or ownership equity in a company. Typically, you source your own deal flow and take full responsibility for conducting due diligence on each company. Afterward, you personally monitor your investments until an exit event. This is the most direct way to become an angel investor, as there are no fees or other parties involved, but also carries the greatest amount of commitment and risk. Remember that it is critical for direct angel investors to create a diversified investment portfolio by investing in multiple companies.

Through an Angel or Seed Fund

An **angel** or **seed fund** is managed by a professional managing partner, and charges a management and incentive fee. The fund typically makes a series of very early investments, meant to support start-ups until they can generate cash of their own, or until they are ready for further investments.

Investors in the fund are known as limited partners. Investing in a seed fund has the benefit of gaining a diversified portfolio of start-ups, as well as a manager to oversee your investment, conduct and source all deal flows, perform due diligence, provide business and strategic guidance, and monitor performance and risk. When investing in a fund, there are additional costs (management fee, carry, fund operating expenses, etc.) charged toward your investment. This lowers your overall return.

An example of an angel or seed fund is the Exxclaim Capital Partners.[24] Exxclaim is a venture capital fund investing in women's health companies across a wide spectrum of health care subsectors. Women have emerged as the largest user of medical products and services, now accounting for 57 percent of the total US health care expenditure. Women also function as the "chief medical officers" of their families, making 80 percent of health care purchasing decisions. As such, there has been an acceleration of women's health-related companies, but traditional venture investment in solutions catering to health and wellness needs of women has lagged. Karen Drexler and her cofounders created a fund to capitalize on this insight.

Participating in a Syndicate

Syndication is a mechanism that allows groups of angels (up to 99) to get small slices of lots of deals. Essentially, a private lead investor creates a syndicate on a site like Angel-List and allows other angels to co-invest in his or her deals. This allows other investors to leverage the lead's due diligence and experience. The syndicate's investment portfolio

---

24   Interview with Karen Drexler.

may be created with specific goals in mind. One example is 500 Startups' 500 Women Syndicate, whose objective is investing $1 million into ten of the top 500 companies with women founders in the next twelve months. The lead investor, 500 Startups, plans to invest $50,000-$100,000. The remainder will be split between syndicate backers, in amounts varying from $250,000-$500,000.

There are a huge variety of syndicates led by seed funds, notable angels, or thematic segments of the start-up space. I personally have invested via a syndicate and found the experience to be terrific. It gave me a chance to network with and learn the angel investing style of the lead investor as well as to leverage the experience of someone with a specific domain expertise. My initial investment size was small, so it made sense to invest via a syndicate and have a more diversified angel investment portfolio.

Because the syndicate is implemented via a fund, there are additional costs (management fee, carry, fund operating expenses, etc.) charged toward your investment. This lowers your overall return.

Investing through an Angel Network

An **angel network** offers a more bottom-up approach to investing in a team. Leadership is less centralized and the responsibilities of due diligence and strategic guidance are shared among all network members. Many angel networks operate with a network fee and a minimum investment requirement, but these tend to be lower than those charged by angel funds. On the other hand, individual responsibility is higher.

An example angel network is 37 Angels, an investor network community of women. The network conducts scheduled pitching summits to introduce new investment opportunities to its members. All members are highly involved throughout the investment process, and make independent investment decisions. Debbie Hidajat, a 37 Angels member, notes that "investing via a network allows one to use a group's knowledge and due diligence to inform one's own investment choices."[25] This also makes building a diversified portfolio easier, as you are benefiting from multiple perspectives and insights.

See facing page for an overview of the four choices.

Angel Investing through Crowdfunding

Equity-based crowdfunding is a relatively new option for angel investors. As Hana describes in detail in Chapter Six, crowdfunding allows entrepreneurs to reach investors to raise funds for their new business ventures and allows investors to purchase an equity stake in the company in return for their investment. It can be a powerful tool for entrepreneurs and a good way for angel investors—especially those who are new to investing—to gain experience while keeping their financial and time commitments manageable.

Risk Aversion and the Confidence Gap

The odds are stacked against women as investors. We earn less and are more likely to have interruptions in our careers. We live longer, but do not work for as many years. All

---

25   Interview with Debbie Hidajat.

	Angel Fund	Syndicate	Network	Direct Angel
Time Commitment	Low, fund conduct due diligence on each start-up, investors conduct due diligence on fund and the management of fund	Medium, leverage due diligence of syndicate lead, potentially some independent due diligence	Medium, team coverage approach to due diligence, leverage network members' expertise	High, individual due diligence of each start-up
Legal Resources Needed	One time review of fund documentations	Review of fund documentation, common terms across all investors of same syndicate round	Review of individual investment terms, may differ across angels	Review of individual investment terms, may differ across angels
Human Capital Contribution	Low	Low	High	High
Financial Contribution Amount	Medium	Low	High/ Medium	High
Diversification	High	Medium	Medium	Low
Fees	Higher, management fee and carry on net performance across all portfolio companies	High, management fee and carry on each start-up	Participation in network fee, usually a minimum investment per year	No management or carry
Return	Returns are on a fund basis, more diversified	Returns will be less than investing directly due to syndicate management and carry fees	Returns are the return on investment of start-up (less any due diligence cost, and legal fees)	Returns are the return on investment of start-up (less any due diligence cost, and legal fees)
Risk Level	Lower	Higher	Higher	Higher

of these factors mean that women require more time to become accredited investors. Even when we do acquire the resources, we are less likely to take that first step into angel investing.

Why is this the case? Studies suggest that women are more risk-averse than men when it comes to investing. BlackRock's Investor Pulse survey even suggests that women's stereotypically lower confidence levels and consensus-driven approaches may put them at a disadvantage, as good returns often require some degree of contrarian thinking[26] (Chapters Two and Seven explore this in more detail).

The Confidence Gap

When it comes to investing, this confidence gap seems to manifest in several different ways. According to a study by Prudential,[27] 20 percent of female breadwinners say they were "very well prepared" to make wise financial decisions, compared with 45 percent of their male counterparts. Blackrock noted that only 35 percent of high-net-worth women compared with 47 percent of high-net-worth men considered themselves wealthy.[28] Merrill Lynch reported[29] that a majority of women say they know less than the

---

26   http://www.blackrockblog.com/2014/02/26/men-women -investment-decisions/

27   http://www.cgsnet.org/ckfinder/userfiles/files/Pru_Women _Study.pdf

28   http://www.blackrockblog.com/2014/02/26/men-women -investment-decisions/

29   http://www.totalmerrill.com/publish/mkt/client/mladvisor/statics/46 _MLWM_2013_Women-Whitepaper_f3-11_15_13-singles.pdf

average investor, while a majority of men say they know more than the average investor. But does this confidence gap really affect the quality of women's investment strategies? Studies suggest no. When you control for things such as wealth levels and investment knowledge, the academic research shows that men and women investors don't actually perform as differently as you might think. Women's lower confidence in their level of preparedness does not indicate an actual lower level of proficiency—it simply reflects a higher level of self-scrutiny.

In fact, women may have several distinct advantages over men when it comes to being smart investors, and particularly smart angel investors. Women tend to be thorough and take more time to make decisions than men. Several studies, including a national survey by LPL Financial,[30] show that women tend to research investments in depth before making portfolio decisions, and that the process tends to take more time. Women also tend to consult their advisors before adjusting their portfolio positioning, whereas men are more prone to market-timing impulses. To gather information, women often prefer group discussions, while men prefer more independent approaches.

A famous six-year study by finance professors Brad Barber and Terrance Odean[31] found that men traded 45 percent more than women. All this trading activity reduced their net returns by 2.65 percentage points a

30 http://www.blackrockblog.com/2014/02/26/men-women -investment-decisions/

31 http://faculty.haas.berkeley.edu/odean/papers%20 current%20versions/individual_investor_performance_final.pdf

year. In contrast, women only lost 1.72 percentage points due to trading. As angel investing often requires a long investment time frame, the increased patience of women investors may be a boon.

Bridge the Gap!

So, if you are hesitant about making the jump into angel investment—don't be! As studies have shown, women sometimes possess a lack of confidence that doesn't actually map to reality. You might actually know more than you think you do. Speak with your financial advisor on what might be a reasonable allocation, and start from there.

Here are some specific ways I got comfortable with the idea of becoming an angel investor. Some of these may help you bridge the confidence gap and make the leap.

Seek a Role Model

Daniela Schreier, clinical psychologist and associate professor at the Chicago School of Professional Psychology, discusses the dynamics of men and women when it comes to investing. "For women, we are generally raised in connection with others. It's very natural for women to hear [about] other people's experience[s] and then place [their] eggs in [the] basket that has turned out profitable returns [for] people [they] trust."[32] This was definitely one of the

32 "Bulls and Bears: How Do Men and Women Compare in Investing?" Chicago Tribune, February 12, 2012 —http:// articles.chicagotribune.com/2012-02-12/business/ct-biz -0212-outside-opinion-male-female-investing-20120212_1_men-and -women-daniela-schreier-financial-adviser

paths I personally took. After the Pipeline Fellowship program, I enrolled in an angel investing class taught by Carol Sands at Stanford University.[33] I have learned so much from Carol's twenty years of angel investing experience and have found incredible mentorship opportunities within the angel investing community.

Connect with and Support Each Other

According to the research of Tahira Hira and Cazilia Loibl in the *Handbook of Consumer Finance Research*, women and men have different ways of learning about investing. "Men are more self-directed learners, using the Internet more than women," says Loibl, an associate professor in the department of consumer science at Ohio State University. "Women rely more on personal networks with friends, family [and] financial planners, and [they] take a networking approach to gathering information. Both [approaches] have positive[s] and negative[s], [but] when we analyzed it to find out if investment outcomes were different, we couldn't find any difference."[34]

I was fortunate to have met an amazing group of women within Wingpact. We support one another and leverage each other's resources tremendously in our joint investments, as well as help each other out with our respective individual investments. We are not alone; the female executives of Twitter have also pooled their collective expertise in angel investing. "Angel investing has

---

33 Carol Sands, Angel Investing for the Serious Investor, Stanford University.

34 Quoted in Bankrate.com - http://www.bankrate.com/finance /investing/investing-styles-men-versus-women-1.aspx

historically been more of a solo sport, and we wanted to adopt a different approach," wrote the founders.[35]

Join an Initiative Such as Wingpact

Angel investing can be a powerful way for women to make a difference, while making a sound personal investment at the same time. This is why we formed Wingpact—a community and network to inspire and mobilize women in angel investing and entrepreneurship.

The Wingpact Initiative will help facilitate the growth of women in angel investing and entrepreneurship with three main objectives that encompass many of the ideas discussed in this chapter:

1. *Investing with a purpose:* finding and focusing on the purpose, social or non-social, that inspires you.

2. *Seeking a role model:* spending time with women who have done angel investing before, and can show you the ropes.

3. *Connecting and supporting:* sharing common experiences, interests, and passions among women angels.

I will invest my portion of this book's proceeds back into women-founded companies.

---

35 http://money.cnn.com/2015/03/05/technology/twitter-angels/

Send the Elevator Back Down

I wish more women would feel empowered to take control of their wealth, and not only work hard themselves, but also make their money work for them. When I decided last year to allocate a portion of my portfolio to angel investing, I was surprised that it quickly became one of the most empowering experiences of my life. That experience inspired me to tell you the story of how I became involved with angel investing and took the first steps to make it happen. I hope that by doing so I can send the elevator back down to you—and pass along that sense of empowerment.

Chapter Four

The Art of Due Diligence and Company Valuation

by Susan Preston

As a founder of Seraph Capital Forum, the first all-women angel investor group in the United States, and a longtime supporter of women entrepreneurs and investors through my prior position at Kauffman Foundation and chair of ARI's Women First Enterprise, my mission for nearly twenty years has been to provide opportunities for women to become more financially confident.

Much has changed in the fifteen years since I founded Seraph—the percentage of women investors has increased; there are more all-women investment groups. Yet much work remains to bring more women into positions of influence. While the ins and outs of investment may seem mystifying to an outsider, an understanding of due diligence and valuation—two essential elements for informed investing—is within anyone's reach. Knowledge, as the saying goes, is power.

Understanding the complexities of due diligence (DD) is essential for any investor and even for entrepreneurs, who understand the importance of being prepared for investor questions. The following discussion provides a good primer for anyone interested in further understanding how to evaluate an early-stage investment opportunity.

The due diligence process, at its most fundamental level, is simply identifying the risks in a deal and then determining if those risks can be eliminated or reduced to insignificance. All early stage deals have risk. That's why they offer low valuations and high upside—or at least they should.

The following discussion provides insights into conducting due diligence that have been learned through the eternal pursuit of the Holy Grail for due diligence. Through analysis of failed and successful investments over many years, certain activities and steps have become apparent that infuse objectivity into the DD process. But don't let anyone fool you: there is no software program that allows you to input twelve factors and spits out an investment decision. You need to put in time and effort to properly analyze a company.

This brings up an important pre-DD step that might save you and the entrepreneur from wasting a lot of time. Let's look at the three pre-DD steps:

1 - Screening

Does the company have your basic and required fundamental attributes? For instance, you invest only in clean tech and this is a mobile application for clothes shopping. Or you require at least a Minimum Viable Product (MVP) and initial customer traction, and this is currently just a cool idea.

2 - Preliminary Due Diligence

If the company meets your basic investment parameters, you will want to conduct some basic diligence, particularly on market size and competitive landscape. You may find that the market is much smaller than the entrepreneur states, which is often the case, not because entrepreneurs inflate the numbers, but because they don't understand how to appropriately define their Total Addressable Market (TAM).[36] To determine TAM, one must understand who the actual customer is. For instance, for a home diabetes monitoring device, the TAM is not the entire health care market, nor even the entire home health care market. Rather, it is the home diabetes monitoring market. So understanding true market size is important.

Competition is another basic DD question. Entrepreneurs rarely identify all their competitors, often because they consider their product or market unique and exceptional. It's striking how often one encounters this perspective among entrepreneurs! They simply don't see many companies as competitors.

When you analyze the competitive landscape, remember to look at the market from the perspective of the *buyer* of the services or product, rather than simply assessing whether the product is cool and innovative. Sometimes people simply don't want or need the newest thing. Their pain is not big enough to warrant a solution. In other words, the product or service is merely a vitamin supplement, not an aspirin for a big headache.

These few hours of preliminary DD not only help you further winnow down the list of possible investments, but also make the investor pitch and first meeting more insightful and thorough than if you came into the meeting unprepared. We coach our entrepreneurs to be prepared for

---

36 TAM or Total Addressable Market is total global revenue opportunity for a product or service, regardless of competition or customer reachability.

that first investor meeting. The reciprocal also holds true: investors should be prepared, too.

Another preliminary DD step you can take, either before or after meeting the entrepreneur and hearing the pitch, is contacting some experts in the field to get their sense of such things as where the market is trending, issues companies encounter, or intellectual property considerations. Academics nearly always enjoy discussing their fields of study and providing their opinions. You also can often find industry-savvy people through your own connections. But be respectful of the entrepreneur's innovation when making these calls and avoid disclosing anything even possibly proprietary. I always do these early calls with no reference to the company I am analyzing. Rather, I ask general questions about the market and technology bleeding edge. As with market and competitive analysis, I am now better informed and ready for a long, instructive session with the entrepreneur.

3 - Basic Terms

You have read through all materials, conducted preliminary DD, heard the pitch, and had a couple of follow-up meetings and/or calls with the entrepreneur. You are still stoked on the technology, team, and market. So it's time to move on to deep and thorough due diligence, right?

Of course you can do so at this point, but I recommend you take this advice from a sage investor: first, seek agreement with the entrepreneur on the basic terms of valuation, investment structure, founder longevity, and post-investment investor engagement.[37] Many times, the entrepreneur already will have expressed preference for a particular investment structure: equity,[38] convertible note, or straight note. If you are fundamentally opposed to the deal structure and the entrepreneur is immovable, you probably shouldn't do the deal—not only because the deal doesn't align with your investment approach, but also because this may signal that the entrepreneur is uncoachable.

On valuation, you need to know if you and the entrepreneur are on the same planet, in the same country, and in the same city, if not the same street. For example, if you consider $2M as a fair valuation for this seed-stage company and the entrepreneur did their friends-and-family round at $20M, or simply believes this is the right valuation, you currently are not on the same planet. You may suggest a convertible note to avoid the valuation question at this time and leave it for the next round of investors with more muscle, but that ultimately just delays facing the issue. You need not agree on the ultimate valuation, but being reasonably close is important. On more than one occasion, I have said goodbye to an entrepreneur because

---

37 *Valuation* refers to both the process of determining the value of a company at the time of investment and to the actual price paid (i.e., $2M). *Investment structure* is the type of investment—debt or equity. Founder longevity relates to the sensitive conversation about how long the founder should remain the CEO. *Post-investment investor engagement* refers to how the investor will interact with the company: passively or actively as an advisor or board member.

38 Equity refers to stock—common or preferred; convertible note refers to a debt instrument that automatically or optionally converts into equity; and a straight note refers to a simple debt instrument.

of discordant valuations, only to find them back in my office a few months later when many other prospective investors have turned them down for the same reason. We will discuss valuation in more detail later in this chapter. Another question you must broach, if applicable, is replacing the founder as CEO. Particularly in the case of engineering and complex technology companies, the founder is often the scientific genius, but not the business expert. Occasionally, a PhD scientist-founder can grow and gain the necessary business acuity (I have a portfolio company with such a CEO), but these are exceptions. Therefore, before launching into full DD, have the honest and sensitive discussion about long-term roles. Many scientific founders are becoming more aware of this issue and lead the conversation themselves, recognizing that we all have our special talents and growing a company requires many different talents and skills. As with the discussion on valuation, approach the topic of shifting roles for the founder with sensitivity and respect.

Finally, you need to have a meeting of the minds with the entrepreneur on your post-investment role. Do you require a board seat or board observation rights, or comprehensive information rights, but the entrepreneur just wants your money without your presence in any form? The entrepreneur may have a fair and reasonable basis for this position, such as a full and capable board, but if their position is inconsistent with yours, consider walking away. Regardless of board or advisory roles, I strongly advise against investing in any company in which the entrepreneur refuses to provide—or expresses great reluctance in providing—minimal information rights of quarterly financials and annual financial and business projections. First, you have a right to know what's happening to your investment, and second, you may be able to help support the company through your contacts and personal experience. Open lines of communication are essential in any relationship, including investor-entrepreneur.

Full Due Diligence: The Details

You have conducted all pre-DD steps and you are still excited about the company's prospects. You like the team and the general terms and valuation range are agreeable. As first pointed out, diligence is about identifying the issues, risks, and solution, or determining that no solution exists. In the latter case, your diligence would conclude with a "no investment" decision. For my own investment portfolio, I invest in about one out of a hundred companies that cross my transom. The vast majority do not make it to full DD. However, many that do are determined not suitable because of various issues discovered through the DD process. Keep in mind, however, that you will never find a seed-stage or start-up company—or a company at any stage of development—without risk. Even publicly traded companies have risks. The process of risk identification for seed- and early-stage companies has more unknowns and a longer list of questions, but part of the fun is learning and discovering, sometimes along with the entrepreneur. Risk is inherent. You simply have to figure out if the risk is resolvable.

Tools and Topics

At the highest level of discussion, all DD can be divided into three overarching categories: market, team, and technology. You can then break these down into subcategories, each of which you should examine and consider in your DD research and analysis. Some people place financial review in a separate category, while I believe it cuts across all categories and impacts all activities. So I have included a separate list of financial DD topics.

The following table gives you an idea of the topics you should cover in discussions and research and diligence calls to get a solid understanding of risk for purposes of making an investment decision:

Technology	Team	Market
• Competition • Intellectual property protection and freedom to operate • Technical risks to final commercial product • Cost of goods • Profit margins at volume production • Cost to develop • Availability of technical talent • Time to commercial product • Manufacturing options (outsourcing)	• Coachability of entrepreneur • Company culture • Founder's leadership style • Gaps in team • Availability of talent • Option pool for employees • Team's experience of previously working together • Advisory board members • Fiduciary board members • Founder prior experience	• Market size (TAM, SAM and SOM: Total Available Market, Serviceable Available Market, and Serviceable Obtainable Market) • First market— domestic or foreign? • Marketing plan • Go-to-market strategy • Fragmented or market concentration in large incumbents • Market pain solving • Likely acquirers • Strategic partners

Financial Considerations

1. Total capital required to profitability, not just this round

2. Value potential at exit

3. Follow-on funding sources

4. Exit scenarios in detail

5. Use of capital in this round and later

6. Prior investors—are they participating?

7. Co-investors

8. Financial model: realistic scaling, good margins, etc.

Example of Questions for the Market Assessment

1. Does the company's product or service address a new or existing market?

2. Is the product or service platform-based, with the opportunity for additional products or services? Or is this potentially a one-trick pony?

3. Does the company have a well-thought-out sales and marketing plan?

4. Does the company have key relationships in place, or is it working on the same, with marketing and/or sales partners?

5. Does the company have or need key joint venture relationships?

6. Is the company focused on the appropriate market development, or are they trying to do too much at one time?

7. Have they chosen the right first market?

8. Does their product or service represent a market push or pull?

9. What is the potential market size?

10. Have they conducted thorough market research to support their financial assumptions, revenue model, and valuation?

11. What is their stage of development? Concept, alpha, beta or shipping?

12. If the company has already introduced its product or service into the market, what is the number of current and potential customers?

13. What is the length of its sales cycle?

14. What are the channels of distribution?

15. Does the company's product or service have a seasonal aspect?

16. Is this a stable market and are COGs (cost of goods sold) stable?

Neither of these lists is exhaustive, but do give a good idea of the various topics you need to analyze.

An equally important aspect of the process is the angel investor group pulled together to share the duties of due diligence. While you can certainly undertake due diligence as a solo effort, conducting proper due diligence can take up to 100 hours. If you choose to conduct due diligence on your own, be realistic about the amount of time you can dedicate and your areas of expertise. Group due diligence allows you to not only share this dedication of time but also to capitalize on the group's collective expertise in various review areas such as financial, industry, marketing, legal, etc.

Create standard lists of questions and information requests for conducting due diligence. Make sure they are comprehensive, because due diligence is a discovery and analysis process for all possible issues. You will have unique questions for each technology but many areas of inquiry are common to all companies (see the list above). Good checklists remind you of topics you need to cover. The entrepreneur is not trying to hide anything, but they are not going to volunteer or supply information unless they know you need it.

Standard Process

Another important practice in due diligence is to have a disciplined, comprehensive process and stick to it. This is another example of a theme running through this discussion: don't take shortcuts. Don't dismiss important steps such as reference calls or the preliminary DD activities. If you have done a comprehensive job and years down the road the company fails for reasons that arise after your investment, you at least have the knowledge that you were thorough. The alternative might be having an issue arise shortly after investing which, if you had known, would discouraged you from investing. Checklists and information requests are a sort of insurance policy that you have asked the questions and obtained the information you need to make an informed decision.

Just as important as comprehensive checklists, questions, and information requests is a standardized process. Again, the process may vary depending on the technology and team, but this process reminds you of all the activities you should conduct. At this stage of DD, you have already heard the company pitch, had several conversations, and conducted research on the market, technology, and team. Other important steps include conducting a site visit to meet key members of the team as well as to talk with junior team members. You want to know the company's culture and how committed all team members are.

Reference Calls

Another important part of your DD process is reference calls. Do ask your entrepreneurs for references, but don't be surprised that all are favorable. In these days of the Internet and business-oriented social media like LinkedIn, it's easy to reach out through your own network to find people who have worked with the entrepreneur and other key team members.

References should include customers or prospective customers. You do need to be respectful of the entrepreneur's relationship with these important early customers, but it's also essential for you to better understand the true nature of the intended or current relationship. Industry calls are important as well. Contact knowledgeable market leaders and talk to them about their pain and desired solution. You should make these calls anonymously, without disclosing the company's name or details of their technology, and ask general questions about a desired solution. Do not accept an entrepreneur's statements about customer and market status. You need to make your own assessment.

Include academic research leaders in your reference calls. Academicians are typically delighted to talk at length about their field of focus and usually have a good understanding of what represents the state-of-the-art. There are also market research and analysis companies such as Forrester, Gartner, and many others. While their reports may be costly, you can often find abstracts or summaries of the findings, or you may determine a report is worth purchasing.

Investment Memo

All this effort needs to be intelligently articulated, particularly if you are conducting joint DD as part of an angel investment group. An effective mechanism is to have a standard form investment memo, which you complete. The standard memo format will help you remember topics to cover, as do your lists and questions. It's a good discipline.

Nondisclosure Agreements

The opinion on nondisclosure agreements (NDAs) spans the spectrum. I never sign an NDA to review all initial documents, including the executive summary, pitch deck, and business plan. Having reviewed thousands of company materials, I cannot possibly keep track of what information I received from whom. Entrepreneurs should not put any information about their "secret sauce" in these documents. If I decide to enter full due diligence, and particularly if there are filed but unpublished patent applications, I will sign an NDA at that time. Some venture capitalists never sign NDAs for the reason above. They hire experts to do the detailed technology review. The expert signs the NDA and then provides a summary analysis and opinion on the technology. The decision about if and when to sign an NDA is your personal choice.

Background Checks

Some investors like to do criminal record and financial (bankruptcy) background checks. It can be important to know if the entrepreneur has had any issues with the Securities and Exchange Commission or has a colorful litigation history. Your DD checklist should include questions about past litigation, bankruptcies, and other legal issues. Even with these questions, some investors like to conduct independent searches.

What's Most Important?

At this time, you may be asking, well, what's really most important? Team? Technology? Market? Having been an investor for fifteen-plus years, I can say with conviction: *everything*. Some people argue that team is most important, as a stellar team can create a win out of an average technology. That is undoubtedly true. But through the years, I have seen companies fail for reasons in all three overarching categories. You simply must give the proper amount of time and attention to each category. As stated before, don't take shortcuts. If you do and the company fails because of what you didn't analyze, you will have a harder time accepting the loss.

Studies have shown a direct correlation between the number of hours committed to due diligence and the eventual return. Professor Wiltbank at Willamette University analyzed hours to ultimate return. The results should not be surprising. In the 2007 *Returns of Angels in Groups*, Professor Wiltbank obtained information from 539 angels in 3,097 investments and included 1,137 exits and closures. He found the following:

- return for DD less than 20 hours = 1.1X

- returns for DD more than 20 hours = 5.9X

- returns for DD more than 60 hours = 7.1X

Have Fun

The DD process is time-consuming and complex, but following a disciplined process is the sign of a great investor. However, this doesn't need to be a tortured task. Learning about a new technology and getting to know a brilliant team can be truly enjoyable. Making an investment is exhilarating and knowing you have done a great job leading up to that moment makes the process gratifying. Enjoy!

Now that we have a better understanding of how to evaluate a company, let's turn to the important and often contentious process of determining what the company is worth at the time of your investment.

Company Valuations

Some people believe the valuation process is akin to throwing darts at a board—blindfolded. Ultimately, the valuation for a funding round is the amount two parties arrive at after an arm's length negotiation. Of course, you can kick the issue down the road to the next financing round by using a convertible note. This process has advantages and disadvantages, which we won't analyze here. The discussion here presupposes you are interested in/committed to a priced round[39] and therefore want to better understand valuation tools and processes. If you are looking at a company with sales and revenue, you can use a number of valuation techniques, including discounted cash flow, book value, or market comparables. But angel investors typically are looking at pre-revenue, presales companies, so the standard valuation tools do not apply. We need to use more creative means.

Keeping in mind the definitive determinant of valuation—a mutually agreed-to value between two parties—the following tools can help you determine a fair and equitable value. The best valuation is one in which the respective parties, entrepreneur and investor, are reasonably content. Neither party should be thrilled, which

---

39   A "priced round" simply means a financing in which you set or establish a current value or worth for the company. Typically associated with an equity round of financing.

indicates the valuation is not fair and you are entering a long-term relationship with one party feeling resentful.

What mechanisms exist for assessing valuation in a start-up company without revenues and active customers? One is a comparative process. What is the average price being paid for start-up, early-stage companies in your region? According to the Angel Resource Institute's Halo Report, the average seed- or early-stage company valuation is about $2.7 million. Of course, valuations vary regionally as well as with various industries. A mobile application in Silicon Valley will probably have a higher valuation than a clean tech deal in the Southeast. This variation in angel investment rounds is reflected in the following graph from the Halo Report and PitchBook.[40]

Median Seed Stage Pre-Money Valuation
Median Valuation Up 20% From 2013, Highest Ever Top Valuation In HALO

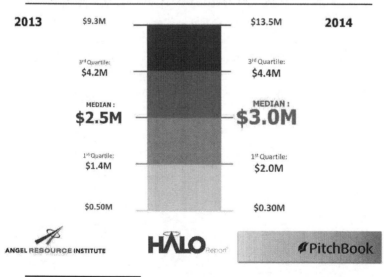

2013			2014
$9.3M			$13.5M
3rd Quartile: $4.2M			3rd Quartile: $4.4M
MEDIAN: **$2.5M**			MEDIAN: **$3.0M**
1st Quartile: $1.4M			1st Quartile: $2.0M
$0.50M			$0.30M

ANGEL RESOURCE INSTITUTE   HALO Report   PitchBook

40   http://www.angelresourceinstitute.org/research/halo
-report/halo-report.aspx

Maintaining an awareness of general valuation trends in your region is an important part of the valuation assessment process. What valuations are other companies at a similar stage in a similar market receiving? Variables such as a serial successful entrepreneur, strong intellectual property position, and other positive factors can provide a premium above the median valuation, but will typically not support a doubling. The extremes in valuation usually reflect geographic and industry sector (what's hot) investor preference.

Comparative Method

With an understanding of your regional valuation trends, you can now assess your prospective investment against that norm. How do the various risks and rewards for this investment compare to a typical investment opportunity? Is the market, as you have verified it, very large, say $500 million? Have the entrepreneurs already built a functional beta product or already launched their Minimum Viable Product? These positive—value-increasing—attributes may be countered by negatives, such as a team that's missing key positions in a tight workforce market with a complicated go-to-market pathway.

What does a typical angel company, one that supports the median regional valuation, look like? Now, how does your prospective investment compare on a number of variables you determine important to consider in arriving at a fair valuation? These factors typically include:

- market size/potential

- completeness of team

- technology—product or services

- management/team

- competition

- go-to-market/sales channel

- other factors, such as first market being foreign

In looking at these factors, consider the relative importance of each for a particular company. Then ask the question: how does this company compare to investable companies in your region? Does it have a better team than the average angel deal? Is the technology more developed than the average deal? Or is there a complicating factor, such as having Europe as the first point of market entry? Also, the presence of large incumbent market players may negatively impact valuation.

You can arrive at a fair valuation through this process of comparing the risks and values of the prospective investment against current angel deals. Of course, this is only one method of determining valuation in a pre-revenue company. Another is the returns method, discussed below.

Venture Capital/Returns Method

Another method for calculating valuation answers the question of whether you can make an adequate return. This method is called the venture capital or returns method, partly because of the VC focus on returns. Desired high returns are not unique to VCs—angels want good returns as well—but historically angels have been perceived as having relatively low expectations or simply not being sophisticated enough to appreciate the need for strong returns. I believe angels are becoming far more sophisticated and desire returns commensurate with their risk exposure. Therefore, we will refer to this valuation method as the returns method of valuation since it's not exclusive to VCs.

As an angel investor, you are aware of the importance of creating a diversified portfolio of investments. Over a lifetime of investing, angel investors should have at least ten to fifteen companies in their portfolio. Angel investing has a high-risk profile because of the many unknowns about the company at the time of investment. Accordingly, angels should receive higher returns for this risk compared to later-stage investors. It also means that more companies are likely to fail. Despite our best efforts in conducting thorough due diligence, identifying all known risks and a pathway to eliminating them, those pathways don't always materialize. And other risks arise or external forces can result in company failure. Thus we need to find companies that offer high returns. I look for companies that can support at least a 10X (ideally 20X) return calculation based on my own assessment of proforma (or projected) financials. If your individual companies have this return potential, then in a blended portfolio (one that also includes both the likely number of companies returning zero along with those returning pennies on the dollar) your big successes could yield an average return at 3X to 4X on your overall portfolio—a definite success.

In assessing the return potential of an individual company, you need to know the total capital requirements for the company to become cash flow positive and for your eventual exit. Each subsequent round of financing will dilute your ownership interest unless you are able to continue investing your pro rata, which is difficult for nearly all angel investors.

The following flow chart gives the steps in determining if an investment is suitable using the returns method. This chart assumes only one round of financing to illustrate the steps. The chart is followed by example comparisons with subsequent funding rounds, which is the norm.

Returns Method

This example assumes a desired return rate of 10X ROI (return on investment)

Investment	$1 million	I am the sole investor for this round, which is all the money the company needs
Exit Year	5th year	Market comparables show acquisitions of companies at the maturation this company will be at in the 5th year
Revenues (5th year)	$20 million	I have made my own assessment of the company's financials and believe this is a fair projection of revenues
Net profits	10% = $2 million	I have decided to look at net profit and do market comparables. I could also use gross income to calculate terminal value
P/E Ratio for industry	15X	I have looked at various Internet sources to arrive at my best estimate of a price-earnings ratio [41]
Company terminal value	$30 million	This is simply the net profit amount of $2 million times the P/E ratio ($2M X 15 = $30M)

Required return	$10 million	As stated above, I need at least a projected 10X return on my investment. Therefore, if I invest $1 million, I need a return of $10 million.
Percentage ownership needed	33%	If the company has a projected terminal value of $30 million, and I need to receive $10 million to get my 10X return, I need to own 33% of the company or $10 million of $30 million
Post-money valuation	$3 million	Since mine is the only investment money, I can easily calculate the valuation I will pay at the time of my investment. Because I need to own 33% of the company at the exit, I need to own 33% at the time of investment.
Pre-money valuation	$2 million	If I invest $1 million, I will achieve my 33% by paying no more than $2 million pre-money valuation. My ownership is based on the post-money valuation, and pre-money plus money invested equals post-money, or in this case $2M to $1M invested = $3M; $1M/$3M = 33%

As you can understand, the model gets more complicated with multiple anticipated rounds at unknown valuations. All you can do under these circumstances is make judgment calls on likely valuations at subsequent

---

41   The P/E ratio is calculated as market value per share/earnings per share. By example, if a company's stock is trading at $50.00 per share and the earnings over the last 12 months were $3.00 per share, the P/E ratio is $50/$3 or 16.7. P/E ratios are regularly tracked for publicly traded companies. To determine an appropriate P/E ratio for calculating Returns Method valuation, look at several comparable companies in the same or similar industry.

rounds. To assist in this process, it is helpful to stay aware of regional and industry values for further rounds of funding. Know what subsequent investors are looking for in terms of company growth that will impact valuation and the possibility of a subsequent round with a new lead investor. During the dot-com bubble, companies and investors could rely on a 3X increase in valuation between each round; for the most part, those days are gone. We occasionally read in the media about extraordinary valuations, but these exceptions should not be used as indicators of the norm. Many factors—from state of the market, completion of technology development, commercialization ramp, strategic partners, etc.—will impact valuation at each stage. Be conservative in your estimate of valuation at each funding stage so your final assessment gives room for upside from company advancement and success.

The following two examples give a simple comparison of the impact of scale and funding requirements:

Example 1:	Example 2:
• $2M investment	• $2M investment
• $2M pre-money valuation	• $2M pre-money valuation on first round
• 50% ownership	
• In 5 years, sell for $40M	• Company needs $15M more
• Investor receives: $20M	• Original investment now only 10% of company
• 10X return	• In 5 years, sell for $40M
	• Investor receives: $4M
	• 2X return

Other valuation methods can include market comparables, which is implied in the two methods discussed above, comparative and returns methods. A growing number of independent Internet-based resources/businesses track private equity valuations. These are typically on venture capital investments, but this information can be valuable for early-stage companies to give an idea of subsequent round valuations. Keep in mind that the few deals venture capitalists do at the seed stage are likely companies they consider particularly hot because of market factors or serially successful entrepreneurs, which will garner a higher-than-normal valuation. Therefore, be sure to understand the context of any company's valuation.

As previously stated, valuation is the amount two people arrive at through arm's length negotiation in which neither party is thrilled but rather just okay. If you are only a few hundred thousand apart from your entrepreneur on a deal north of $2 million, it may create a lot of goodwill with your entrepreneur if you give them their valuation. In the long run, that small percentage will, one hopes, not impact you greatly and the strengthened relationship will provide a long-term benefit.

As a concluding thought, some of your best information comes from other experienced angel investors in your region. Networking with other investors and professionals such as lawyers and accountants in the early-stage market keeps you apprised of valuation and deal term trends. Active angel investing requires much more than just assessing deals. Being a savvy investor means being informed and connected. It will pay off.

Chapter Five

Looking Beyond the Horizon: the State of Angel Investing in Emerging Economies

by Christine Emilie Lim

While seasoned angel investors abound, particularly in developed economies, there is opportunity for angels to look into start-ups in developing markets. As when they invest in the public markets, angels face challenges in emerging countries that struggle with political strife and economic issues, such as poverty and lack of quality education and resources. The investing infrastructure is nascent, and angel investors may find themselves at the leading edge of change and growth.

In this chapter, entrepreneurs and investors from Egypt, Argentina, Venezuela, and the Philippines weigh in on the challenges they faced and the rewards they reaped in their respective countries. We also examine the challenges of start-up funding in developing markets and the opportunities to bring women into the conversation.

Traditional Businesses Still Dominate and Entrepreneurs Struggle

In most emerging markets, local entrepreneurs still focus on traditional brick-and-mortar businesses, such as exporting, retail, and manufacturing, for which bank loans are the go-to way to raise capital.

Argentina's many entrepreneurs struggle with this funding conundrum. According to Lilian Lanzieri, who runs a public relations firm, most Argentine entrepreneurs remain in business fewer than four years. The most likely explanations are lack of a sound business plan and scarce funding. According to EY G20 Entrepreneurship Barometer 2013, 88 percent of entrepreneurs surveyed in Argentina believe that it is difficult to access funding in their country, compared to 70 percent across the G20, which comprises a mix of the world's largest advanced and emerging economies.[42]

Growth of Companies Seeking Angel and Venture Funding

Funding traditional businesses through venture capital or through angel investors is a new concept, and one that has been slow to develop. Instead, nontraditional new businesses—notably technology start-ups—have become a key driver for angel networks and venture capitalists, especially from neighboring developed countries, to enter emerging

---

42 EY G20 Country Report 2013: Argentina, http://emergingmarkets.ey.com/wp-content/uploads/downloads/2013/09/EY-G20-country-report-2013-Argentina.pdf. The report factors in (1) ease of business, (2) business regulations, (3) labor market rigidity, such as the cost of firing and (4) taxation.

markets. These technological projects require less capital and are less exposed to local economic problems because their customers or users could easily reach the global market.

The Philippines offers an example of how things are changing. Paul Rivera, CEO/Cofounder of Kalibrr, a start-up providing a talent management platform, says that the Philippine start-up ecosystem has seen a recent influx of cash. This phenomenon has accelerated over the last twelve months with the creation of several venture capital, angel funds and accelerators targeted either to the Philippines or the Southeast Asia region, such as Monk's Hill Ventures and Golden Gate Ventures.

The picture is similar in Latin America. In 2013, venture capital investors active in Latin America deployed US$425 million. This represents more than four times the amount invested when the Latin America Private Equity and Venture Capital Association[43] began collecting data in 2008, and a 15 percent increase from 2012.

Silvia Carbonell, director of the Center for Entrepreneurship and professor in New Venture and Entrepreneurship for the IAE Business School in Argentina, has worked as an entrepreneur since 1998. When she began eighteen years ago, nobody knew about risk or venture capital. Even today, both high potential entrepreneurs and investors are still getting educated, with new private and public initiatives in place.

---

43   http://www.lavca.org

Lack of Education and Misinformation about Investing are Barriers

Despite all the momentum in developing economies, many entrepreneurs still lack knowledge—and are sometimes misinformed—about important basics of entrepreneurship and funding, such as raising money, valuing a business, giving equity to advisors or investors, or offering the appropriate vehicle for a particular investor, whether through a convertible note or equity. According to Kalibrr's Rivera, most local Filipino entrepreneurs are uneducated about the process, while expatriate entrepreneurs are more skilled at raising seed funding at good valuations. Many local investors are also raising seed capital for the first time. The fact that they are not yet seasoned investors puts them at a disadvantage.

For example, Noha Mahmound of the Cairo-based technology start-up accelerator Juicelabs finds that legalities and terms sheets are new concepts for both start-up founders and investors, often making the funding process inefficient and unnecessarily lengthy. Usually, negotiations fall through.

Lack of Legal Transparency Makes Funding Convoluted

The lack of transparency within the legal structure in these developing economies makes the funding process convoluted, causing many mistakes and frustration. For instance, convertible note financing, which is common for early-stage start-ups, is treated differently in other

countries compared to the US. In the Philippines, investors are liable for taxes for any paper gains in the value
of their investment. Generally, Filipino incorporation
laws are not very start-up-or foreign-friendly since many
industries restrict the percentage of foreign ownership. As
a result, many start-ups operating in the Philippines have
chosen to incorporate in neighboring Singapore or even in
Delaware, as Kalibrr has.

A New Breed of Investors

Carbonell points out that a different set of angel investors
is entering the ecosystem in these developing markets.
These investors seek not only to diversify their portfolio
of investments, but also to be a part of the movement
towards innovation, social impact, and entrepreneurship.
They are willing to get involved despite political corrup-
tion, unwieldy bureaucracy, the weakness of the rule of
law, high taxes, and other obstacles. These investors have
a higher risk tolerance and aim to diversify their angel
investments by investing or joining country-specific
angel networks.

Accelerators and local angel networks have sprouted
to support the new crop of technology start-ups, with the
goal of prescreening, mentoring, incubating, and ultimately
funding potential start-ups at the seed round. These incubators also provide quality deal flow for investors. For example,
Wayra, one of Latin America's largest accelerator programs,
and the Philippines' Ideaspace and Kickstart Ventures, both
of which are operated by two of the largest conglomerates
in the country, are actively seeking out the next big thing
in their respective countries. Angel groups such as Cairo
Angels, Manila Angels (founded by Rivera), and Argentina's

first Business Angel Club (founded by Carbonell) offer mentorship programs and provide local entrepreneurs the chance to pitch members of the angel group.

Strategic Investing for Diaspora Communities and Social Impact

Large funding institutions are taking note of investing challenges in these areas. The Rockefeller Foundation and the Aspen Institute are giants in their respective areas of economic advancement and educational/policy studies. In February of 2014, these organizations launched the Rockefeller Aspen Diaspora (RAD) Initiative. RAD's primary goal is to more effectively channel investments from diaspora communities into their countries of origin since global remittances dwarf foreign assistance by a factor of three and total $414 billion.[44] During the current exploratory pilot phase, RAD is focusing on US diaspora communities originating from Colombia, Egypt, India, Kenya, and the Philippines.

Social impact investors are drawn to emerging markets. Impact investing is another way to improve the lives of the less fortunate and to unlock substantial for-profit investment capital to complement philanthropy. The Rockefeller Foundation also believes that Southeast Asia is the next hub for impact investing.[45] The need for capital is particularly urgent in the region, where hundreds of millions lack access to education, clean water, and other elements critical to their well-being. Reportedly, there are $10 trillion in combined assets among

---

44   http://www.aspeninstitute.org/policy-work/RAD/about-rad

45   http://www.rockefellerfoundation.org/blog/southeast-asia -next-hub-impact

high-net-worth individuals in Southeast Asia.[46] Mobilizing even 1 percent of this amount for impact investing would make a significant difference.

With Challenges Come Opportunities

Even in emerging countries where angel networks exist, accessing them can be difficult for entrepreneurs who don't have a wide array of business associations or don't belong to the upper class of the society. Entrepreneurs can mitigate these challenges by attending meetups and conferences, such as Geeks on a Beach in the Philippines and Tech in Asia Conference, to meet local and global investors. Crowdfunding sites, such as AngelList, are another avenue to reach international investors, as discussed in Chapter Six.

Alejandro Quintero, CEO and cofounder of Cuestiona.me, a Venezuela-based question-and-answer online platform, has found business traction in his home country and in Columbia. However, he has been less successful in attracting local investors. In order to scale, he needed to come to the United States to hone his business plan under Manos Accelerator, an accelerator program for Latino entrepreneurs.

The US-based Manos Accelerator launched the first and only accelerator in Silicon Valley targeted to Latino entrepreneurs in the fall of 2014. Its Manos Angel Network and angel investing bootcamp program, Manos Angel Bootcamp, both aim to address the lack of education

---

46   http://www.socialenterprisebuzz.com/2013/03/26/the
-rockefeller-foundation-creates-dedicated-fund-for-social-enterprise
-and-impact-investing-growth-in-asia

about investment and the dearth of knowledgeable local angel investors in Latin America. Angel investors-in-training undergo an intensive training program to learn about the start-up due diligence process, including business valuation, funding vehicles, exit strategies, financial assessment, and negotiation tactics.

Governments are Slowly Stepping Up

Public or government initiatives also have been assisting local entrepreneurs, albeit at a slower pace than many private undertakings. For instance, in May of 2014, the Philippine senate filed the Startup Business Bill (Senate Bill 2217) with the goal of exempting start-ups from taxes in the first two years of operation.[47]

The government of Buenos Aires has instituted programs, such as the National Program for Young Entrepreneurs, to give entrepreneurs easier access to funding, foster entrepreneurship culture, and provide education and training. Its so-called "Godmothers" initiative aims to build alliances between young entrepreneurs and established companies.[48] There are also courses for entrepreneurs on how to raise seed funding, some of which are even promoted by the Argentinean government. Silvia Carbonell points to the government's investment in four accelerators that provide seed capital as evidence of public sector support.

---

47   http://www.senate.gov.ph/lis/bill_res.aspx?congress =16&q=SBN-2217

48   EY G20 Country Report 2013: Argentina, http://emergingmarkets .ey.com/wp-content/uploads/downloads/2013/09/EY-G20-country -report-2013-Argentina.pdf

The Gender Divide Persists

Despite the steady increase of local entrepreneurs and savvier investors, the same gender gap that bedevils established markets persists in the demography of investors in emerging countries. Most angel investors are male, have been educated overseas, or are expatriates with extended capital.

Noha Mahmound, of Juicelabs tech accelerator, has worked with around fifty investors in Egypt, most of whom are in their mid-thirties or older, are well-traveled, have graduated from school and worked overseas, or are successful lawyers and businessmen who want to help with due diligence and mentoring. The majority of these investors, who have had no formal training in angel investing, are part of the Egyptian diaspora with a gender ratio of 30 percent female to 70 percent male.

Similarly, Kalibrr CEO Paul Rivera identified most angels in the Philippines as male. Mostly educated overseas, they are successful entrepreneurs or come from families with wealth, and are in their thirties to early forties. Most do not have work experience in the technology industry but are involved in finance, outsourcing, manufacturing, and importing/exporting and are relatively new to angel investing as an asset class.

Similar Patterns in Developing Countries

As the start-up ecosystem matures in developing countries, we will most likely see the same pattern that has emerged in developed economies, in which males dominate the funding ecosystem. Companies with women on their executive teams account for less than 5 percent of all ventures receiving equity capital, according to the Diana Project: Women Entrepreneurs 2014.[49] This funding inequity will persist if women investors do not step up in these developing countries.

This is where the opportunity side of the equation comes in. Angel investors interested in impact investing have the potential to change the investing landscape in developing countries. The small number of women-owned ventures receiving funding represents a great opportunity in emerging markets. If women begin to consider angel investing in these markets, then change can begin to occur alongside the change that is happening in developed markets.

Of course, before delving into angel investing in developing markets, you'll need to consider these factors: your investment risk tolerance, skills and industry experience that can be valuable to local entrepreneurs, business knowledge of a specific developing country or region, and your role as an investor—some of which you can learn about in this book.

Chapter Six

Leveling the Playing Field: Crowdfunding as a Stepping Stone to Angel Investing

by Hana Yang

Did you ever wonder how some people can talk about their investments so matter-of-factly and freely? Did you ever wish you could be part of these discussions?

Did you ever hunger for the knowledge that seems to come so easily to those who have accumulated wealth?

Have you thought about becoming an entrepreneur or using your resources to support entrepreneurs? If you have "made it" financially, have you ever wondered how you might make an impact beyond your philanthropic dollars? Have you longed to create change in the world by identifying, improving, and supporting the underserved?

Did you ever wish these questions were more universally acknowledged and the answers more widely known, accessible, shared, and even celebrated?

One way to find answers is to pack up your bags and go in search of them. This is exactly what I did when I moved—alone—from Argentina to Kansas at age fifteen in 1998 to learn English; to Southern California in 1999 to pursue a better education; to Northern California in 2002 to resolve my identity crisis; to New York in 2007 to discover that I, too, could do meaningful and mission-aligned work; and back to Silicon Valley in 2011 to immerse myself in the hub of innovation so I could revolutionize industries—and myself. After all those meandering years, I finally arrived at a strong sense of my own courage. And I found a desire to start embracing my past, embodying my present, and looking forward to my future. It was in Silicon Valley where I truly felt like a lightbulb or two turned on.

Roaming the globe isn't an option for everyone with a hunger to better themselves and change the world. Another approach is to discover tools that will help you find answers. I did this, too, as when I stumbled on the relatively new funding method called *crowdfunding* after years of struggling to innovate in an underserved world via the nonprofit fund-raising sector.

How I Arrived Here

Growing up with limited information and limited access to resources forced me to seek both knowledge and resources for survival. I became naturally hungry to know everything that was both easily available and beyond my reach. Once I figured things out, I naturally wanted to share what I had learned with others in the same boat. This has been my attitude since I left Puerto Iguazu, a small, indigenous—and at the time resourceless—town, home to the famous waterfalls at the intersection of Argentina, Brazil, and Paraguay. I was the only Asian in town at the time. When European and American tourists approached me among my group of friends and spoke to me in English to ask for directions, expecting that I would understand and speak the language, it dawned on me that people were expecting more out of me. Perhaps I was supposed to be a master of the English language. So I decided to head to the middle of America, the most purely American and least culturally diverse place in the country, and enrolled myself in boarding school to start my high school years.

After college, I started my career in 2006 in management consulting. I will always be grateful for that opportunity, since I credit much of the skill, knowledge, and flexibility I have today to that initial career choice. Management consulting provides access to all types of industries, exposure to different types of projects (strategic, implementation, project management), and various levels of team and client interaction, from juniors all the way to C-level executives. This diverse experience let me pick up skills on the job, make connections, and travel to various places in the world for client projects—a pretty sweet way to kick off a professional career for a twenty-one-year-old.

By late 2007, the sub-prime mortgage crisis and subsequent economic downturn in the United States and the rest of the world meant that almost all the projects I was assigned to centered around cost-reduction. I wasn't finding meaning and purpose in my work and knew that I needed to look for something different, with an organization more aligned with what I believed in—access, equal opportunities, and leveling the playing field—and with greater purpose and impact.

I didn't know much about the other side of the for-profit world, the nonprofit sector, beyond some experience volunteering for nonprofit organizations during my high school and college days. But I went where my heart led me with as much hope and conviction as I'd had when I left Argentina nearly ten years earlier. For the first time, I sat down to think through how I might make an impact and leave the world a little bit better place by working in the nonprofit sector. At the time, I thought that was the only option. I observed how passionately people spoke of their causes and nonprofit missions. I asked folks from the industry for advice and learned that fund-raising was key in sustaining and carrying a nonprofit's mission. I wanted to be at the forefront of it all—mobilizing resources for the nonprofit sector and everyone in it. But first I wanted to become a master at it.

After months of market research among my contacts at Junior Achievement, Rotary Club, and local churches, I decided to become a subject matter expert in nonprofit fund-raising management. It felt like the right choice, given my soft skills—being passionate and a people person—and hard skills from my consulting background. I envisioned eventually working in an international setting with global impact such as the United Nations. I wanted to do it right and I wanted to do it all. I entered a graduate degree program in nonprofit fund-raising at Columbia University.

Once in the program, I ran to be president of the Fund-raising Student Association (FSA) and had an opportunity to lead a roundtable on social media strategy for fund-raising for the FSA student members. The event completely changed my perspective on what I aspired to do. It became clear that part of my calling was to bring the digital age, innovation, and technology into the fund-raising sector.

As soon as school was over, I moved three years' worth of my belongings out of my tiny Manhattan studio apartment into a white Hyundai Santa Fe SUV. Without thinking twice, on the snowiest day of the year, I drove back west towards Silicon Valley. I had no idea what to expect. I had no background in technology, but I knew for sure that I was ready to take on a new challenge. Nothing was going to stop me, not even the snowstorm that shut down New York City on December 26, 2010.

I made the jump into technology by working first at Adobe, where I learned the basics of how tech companies work. Then I did what everyone comes to do in Silicon Valley: I joined a promising start-up.

The start-up I joined, Fundly, is a donations-based crowdfunding platform and for me it was a dream come true. Fundly was growing quickly when I first learned of the company. Nonprofits as well as individuals were running fund-raising campaigns on the platform. Given its nimble start-up stage, Fundly had been serving both the B2C (business-to-consumer) and B2B (business-to-business) segments. I had the opportunity to join the B2B team and work with large, established nonprofits such as Habitat for Humanity International, the US Olympics Committee, Indiana University, and the Arnold Palmer Children's Hospitals (to name just a few) on meeting their six- or even seven-digit fund-raising goals. I was with Fundly for an exhilarating ten-month roller-coaster ride during which the company grew, pivoted, experienced ups and downs, and finally decided to refocus on its B2C segment. The B2B team, of which I was a part, had to leave because the company was no longer focusing on the B2B segment.

Fundly did well with its focus back on the B2C market. It is still going strong in San Francisco with the rest of the hottest start-ups in Silicon Valley and was recently acquired. As for me, I wouldn't trade my roller-coaster experience with a Silicon Valley start-up for anything. I believed not only in the solution we were offering, the disruption we were creating, and the lives we were impacting, but also in the team behind it. My experience at Fundly gave me more strength and courage to go outside of my comfort zone and take on new opportunities.

I have become passionate about fund-raising, and in particular, crowdfunding, not only because it plays such a huge role in the ability of an organization to carry out its mission—through storytelling and the wide reach of the fundraisers' networks—but also because it encourages the marginalized to realize their dreams while democratizing funding and giving everyone an opportunity to tell their story. The playing field becomes truly leveled when anyone, regardless of age, race, gender, socioeconomic status, or religion, can provide as well as receive support.

Exciting Times for Women, Exciting Times for Crowdfunding

If there were ever a segment of society that could benefit from a level playing field, it's women. Despite making up more than half the world's population, women still have far fewer opportunities to build wealth and exercise power. But these are exciting times, with increased interest in women's entrepreneurship and an accompanying plethora of resources, services, media coverage, and overall support from the bottom up (the masses), the top down (leadership), and from everyone in-between.

Similar disruption, interest, and activity have occurred in the crowdfunding space. Both women and crowdfunding disruptions are here to stay and are making great impact across a range of industries. Crowdfunding will continue to evolve into a mainstream funding option. The women's entrepreneurial ecosystem will undergo a similar (r)evolution, so women eventually will end up on a more level playing field. I believe these two evolutions are inevitable. And women entrepreneurs are already having early success with crowdfunding[50]—a truly exciting development.

It's not just wealthy women who can fund women entrepreneurs, as Ventureneer founder and president Geri Stengel has pointed out. Certain types of crowdfunding, such as rewards-based (described later in this chapter), enable anyone to invest in anyone. In this context, crowdfunding is a natural fit for women who have become power users of the Internet and social media—two skills that are key to successfully raising money from the crowd.[51]

Crowdfunding made its way into this book because I believe in the power of the crowd—its ability to empower both the owner of the fund-raising campaign (the entrepreneur, creator, or fund-raiser) as well as the supporter (the investor, backer, or funder). Crowdfunding becomes a truly democratic tool because *everyone* and *anyone* can now access funding. No other model has been able to so quickly overcome long-ingrained cultural and even political norms to offer this kind of near-instant democratization

---

50   *11 Reasons 2014 Will Be A Breakout Year for Women Entrepreneurs* http://www.forbes.com/sites/geristengel/2014/01/08/11-reasons -2014-will-be-a-break-out-year-for-women-entrepreneurs/

51   *11 Reasons 2014 Will Be A Breakout Year for Women Entrepreneurs* http://www.forbes.com/sites/geristengel/2014/01/08/11-reasons -2014-will-be-a-break-out-year-for-women-entrepreneurs/

of access to financial and human capital. If you embrace it now, you may even help determine what crowdfunding will become and how it will power causes and new companies and empower entrepreneurs and angel investors.

For this book's audience of potential angel investors, this chapter focuses on what the current crowdfunding landscape looks like; what role crowdfunding plays for seasoned or sophisticated angel investors; the pros and cons of using crowdfunding for angel investing; and the best way to get involved in angel investing via a crowdfunding platform. This information is intended for both new and aspiring angels as well as angel investors who are new to the crowdfunding space.

I feel as if I have arrived at the junction of two great forces at exactly the right time, with the right background and tools, to finally make a difference in the way I had hoped since I packed my bags and went in search of answers many years ago. The remainder of this chapter brings that knowledge to any woman who wants to empower herself to make a difference in the world through crowdfunding.

Introducing Crowdfunding

Definition of Crowdfunding

Crowdfunding is the tool, practice, and process used to fund an initiative by raising small individual financial contributions from a group online and through social media.[52] More formally, crowdfunding serves as an alternative source of capital to support a wide range of

---

52 http://www.investopedia.com/terms/c/crowdfunding.asp

ideas and ventures. An entity or individual raising funds through crowdfunding typically seeks small individual contributions from a large number of people. A crowdfunding campaign generally has a specified target amount for funds to be raised, or goal, and an identified use of those funds. Individuals interested in the crowdfunding campaign—members of the crowd—may share information about the project, cause, idea, or business with each other and use the information to decide whether or not to fund the campaign based on the collective wisdom of the crowd.[53] Put more simply, crowdfunding uses the power of the Internet and social media to raise small amounts of money from lots of different people.[54]

Types of Crowdfunding

This chapter focuses on *equity-based crowdfunding*, since it is most relevant to shaping the new fund-raising and investing economy for women entrepreneurs and angel investors. However, there are four main types of crowdfunding platforms and practices:

1. **Donation-based.** Nonprofits and political groups typically use this type of crowdfunding for their fund-raising campaign efforts. Organizations are able to further promote their mission, solicit donations, reengage with past and existing constituents, identify

---

53   Securities and Exchange Commission: http://www.sec.gov/rules/proposed/2013/33-9470.pdf

54   *11 Reasons 2014 Will Be A Breakout Year for Women Entrepreneurs* http://www.forbes.com/sites/geristengel/2014/01/08/11-reasons-2014-will-be-a-break-out-year-for-women-entrepreneurs/

new constituents by reaching out to the networks of their existing networks, and receive donations online. Think of traditional fundraisers for good causes such as walk-a-thon events, disaster relief campaigns, or even friends and family who may want to make contributions in honor of a deceased loved one. Fundly, GoFundMe, and FirstGiving, among others, are examples of donation-based crowdfunding platforms. A well-known nonprofit, Habitat for Humanity International, runs its crowdfunding campaigns for local and international home builds on the Fundly platform.

2. **Reward-based.** This is similar to donation-based crowdfunding but with the addition of a perk for contributors or funders. Creative projects and new business ventures in need of financial backing feature their projects or products, engage with a mission-aligned community online, and receive funding to complete the project or develop the product. In return, funders receive a product or service as a reward once the campaign is successfully completed. The best known reward-based platforms are Indiegogo and Kickstarter. GoldieBlox, which promotes and develops early interest in STEM (Science, Technology, Engineering, Math) education, and Oculus Rift, a virtual reality headset for 3D gaming, are examples of a couple of the successful reward-based crowdfunding campaigns run on Kickstarter.

3. **Debt-based.** This is peer-to-peer lending to businesses and individuals in return for interest payments. Prospective borrowers submit information about their

loan needs through an online application process that ensures they meet certain criteria. Individuals who turn to debt-based platforms might include people who want to consolidate their debt (by, for example, paying off credit card debt) or obtain specific financing such as for fertility treatments to start a family.[55] Lenders can be individuals or institutions. This form of crowdfunding also is gaining popularity as a funding tool, through platforms such as Funding Circle, Lending Club, and Prosper.[56]

4. **Equity-based.** This type of crowdfunding platform enables entrepreneurs to reach investors to raise funds for their new business ventures and allows investors to purchase an equity stake in the company in return for their investment. With an equity stake, investors may have ownership and/or voting rights. Many equity-based crowdfunding platforms strive to facilitate the vetting of new business ventures by curating their own portfolios and helping investors mitigate investment risk. This type of crowdfunding is more conducive to venture financing than the other forms of crowdfunding. As of Oct. 30, 2015, both accredited and nonaccredited investors can invest in companies using equity-based crowdfunding platforms. This rule

---

55 Lending Club Success Stories: https://www.lendingclub.com /public/borrower-stories-br.action

56 Debt-Based Crowdfunding: The Other Investment Opportunity: http://www.crowdclan.com/debt-based-crowdfunding-investment -opportunity/

is known as Regulation A+[57] and is a huge milestone for equity-based crowdfunding. (More on regulations later in this chapter.) Examples are CircleUp, WeFunder, and Crowdfunder.

To summarize in simpler terms, the major difference among the four types of crowdfunding platforms is that donation-, reward-, and debt-based crowdfunding are not heavily regulated by the Securities and Exchange Commission, while equity-based crowdfunding is.

Where Crowdfunding Fits

Crowdfunding, a sixteen-billion dollar global market in 2014[58] and with projections to reach ninety-three billion by 2025,[59] has assumed a significant role in major sectors in the last five years—from nonprofit and political fund-raising, to backing of creative projects in the entertainment or life-style segments, to funding of entrepreneurial businesses through debt-based crowdfunding. Undeniably, it has also had an impact on the world of entrepreneurship and angel investing for women. According to Ventureneer founder and president Geri Stengel, crowdfunding is a part of the new crowdfinancing sector, which, she says, "provides

---

57   www.sec.gov/news/pressrelease/2015-49.html and Regulation A+: What It Means For Crowdfunding: http://www.businessnewsdaily .com/7920-jobs-act-regulation-a-plus.html

58   Crowdfunding Nearly Tripled Last Year, Becoming a $16 Billion Industry: http://www.entrepreneur.com/article/244503

59   The Crowdfunding Investment Market Will Reach $93 Billion by 2025: https://geobrava.wordpress.com/2014/01/01/the -crowdfunding-investment-market-will-reach-93b-by-2025/

access to money beyond the traditional debt and equity products that are funded primarily by institutions. Instead, it uses peer-to-peer and peer-to-business lending as well as equity-crowdfunding."[60]

Why Crowdfunding Appeals to Women

Crowdfunding offers the potential for a radical evolution of our largely institutional framework for allocating capital. Given women's traditional lack of access to these institutions—foundations, funds, and banks—crowdfunding can play a key role in the women's entrepreneurial ecosystem, offering a more individually driven and direct investment framework accessible to more people.[61] Crowdfunding for businesses[62] has the potential to democratize the private equity market by serving as a means for both women entrepreneurs and women investors to participate more fully in early-stage funding. As the SEC fully implements Regulation A+, we have yet to see how and how soon new and existing investors will adopt this new instrument and how women will actively participate in this kind of equity-based crowdfunding in the longer term, either as investors or as entrepreneurs raising funds. However, evidence from other

---

60 *How Women Are Using Crowdfinancing to Redefine Wall Street*   http://www.forbes.com/sites/geristengel/2014/01/22/how-women-are-using-crowdfinancing-to-redefine-wall-street/

61 *How Women Are Using Crowdfinancing to Redefine Wall Street*   http://www.forbes.com/sites/geristengel/2014/01/22/how-women-are-using-crowdfinancing-to-redefine-wall-street/

62 Crowdfunding's Potential for the Developing World http://www.funginstitute.berkeley.edu/sites/default/files/WB_CrowdfundingReport-ES%20%281%29.pdf

types of crowdfunding platforms demonstrate enormous potential for the involvement of women in the equity-based crowdfunding space.[63] According to Portfolia founder Trish Costello, crowdfunding creates a whole new class of women investors, which manifests itself as a consumer entrepreneurial investing phenomenon. "At the end of the day, funding is the most powerful thing to do for women to get their ideas off the ground," says Deborah Jackson, member of the angel group Golden Seeds and founder of the crowdfunding platform Plum Alley.[64]

Crowdfunding offers a way to enter the angel investing space with minimum emotional and financial commitment. If you are new to angel investing, you may find crowdfunding a good way to get accustomed to the idea of investing. At the same time, you shouldn't rely solely on crowdfunding to build a successful portfolio. Crowdfunding is not a replacement for angel investing and the two are by no means interchangeable. Rather, they are complementary—you will see how in the remainder of the chapter.

Interestingly, but not surprisingly, rewards-based crowdfunding campaigns led by women have a higher success rate in meeting their funding goals than those led by men. According to research by Ventureneer cited in *Crowdfund Insider*, "Women are also outperforming men on specific equity and rewards-based crowdfunding platforms. This is

---

63   Top 10 Crowdfunding Sites for Fundraising http://www.forbes .com/sites/chancebarnett/2013/05/08/top-10-crowdfunding-sites-for -fundraising/

64   The crowdfunding site out to change how many women-led businesses get funded: http://www.fastcompany.com/3034142 /strong-female-lead/the-crowdfunding-site-out-to-change-how -many-women-led-businesses-get-fun

the first evidence that women outshine men when raising financing."[65] Female entrepreneurs are definitely taking advantage of crowdfunding platforms and are drawing attention to and achieving success in their campaigns. Another *Crowdfund Insider* article says, "According to CircleUp, female business leaders are almost ten times more successful in raising capital with online platforms than with traditional banks, and five times more successful compared to their venture capital investments."[66] In its early and potentially less risky stage, reward-based crowdfunding can help expand the pipeline of female investors as the number of female entrepreneurs continues to increase.

To help you understand the role crowdfunding might play in the women's entrepreneurial ecosystem, the next section looks at the nuts and bolts of this financing mechanism.

Impact of Different Kinds of Crowdfunding for Entrepreneurs

In just the few short years since crowdfunding entered the scene, all kinds of people seem to have embraced it. These include

- small grassroots and established nonprofit organizations looking to tap into millennials and the digital generation to boost their donation goals

---

65   http://www.crowdfundinsider.com/2015/04/67012-ventureneer -reports-crowdfunding-for-female-entrepreneurs-to-surpass-male -counterparts-in-securing-funding-driving-revenue-growth

66   http://www.crowdfundinsider.com/2015/07/71191-crowdfunding -is-changing-the-female-entrepreneurial-landscape/

- entrepreneurs seeking backing for projects and companies
- curious individuals who want to get into the investing game and are experimenting by following and sometimes even investing along with well-known investors
- forward-thinking angel investors and venture capitalists looking to source potential deals

A crowdfunding platform today provides two of the elements most essential to both investors and entrepreneurs: access and opportunity. For investors, crowdfunding platforms provide additional deal flow volume and efficient mechanisms to review their investments, quickly communicate with entrepreneurs, and streamline the investment decision-making process.[67] For entrepreneurs, crowdfunding also provides additional access to investors, promotion of their products or companies, tracking of investors or investments, and a more robust way of managing the entire process at scale.

Crowdfunding for Angel Investors

Not only has equity-based crowdfunding become a hot topic, it also has raised forty times more per company than any other type of crowdfunding in the marketplace.[68] This makes it particularly interesting and relevant to angel investors.

---

67 Why Venture Capitalists Are Turning to Crowdfunding: http://www.entrepreneur.com/article/240984

68 Equity Crowdfunding 101: Is It Right For Your Startup? http://www.forbes.com/sites/ericwagner/2014/03/18/equity-crowdfunding-101-is-it-right-for-your-startup/

In the context of this chapter, I define *sophisticated angel* as those who are active and experienced and who qualify as accredited investors[69] under the SEC rule 505 and 506 of Regulation D.[70] *Unsophisticated* investors are both accredited and unaccredited investors who are new to angel investing and crowdfunding. In either case, this chapter is aimed at individuals who are able to provide both financial and human capital to the start-up companies they plan to invest in—those with financial resources, business expertise, mentorship capacity, the ability to provide access to their networks, and who are passionate and interested in working closely with entrepreneurs. These kinds of investors often have a goal not only of generating high returns through their angel investments but also of helping entrepreneurs realize their dreams of transforming the world into a better place through their start-up company ideas.

Crowdfunding and Risk Tolerance

If you are new to angel investing and want to get into the game, you may not have a clear understanding of your own risk tolerance. I recommend starting with reward-based crowdfunding. This can be a great way to dip your toes into the crowdfunding waters by donating to or backing a person or project. Reward-based crowdfunding is a great way for women with financial resources to become

---

69   In general, people with a net worth (excluding their residence) of $1 million, income of $200,000 a year (or $300,000 with their spouse), officers and directors of the issuer and various institutions that have more than $5 million in assets.

70   Accredited investor definition: http://www.sec.gov/answers /accred.htm

comfortable with angel investing because the funding you provide for the inventor or entrepreneur comes with practically no risk at this stage. While the reward you receive in return is not technically a return on your investment—it's more like an online prepurchase order—it can still help you get comfortable with the idea of putting money into a venture that is less than 100 percent certain. As angel investor and coauthor of this book Wingee Sin puts it, "There is no [financial] return with reward-based crowdfunding; it's simply allocating capital towards an initiative that is worthwhile and [she] ha[s] a passion for, and then receiving goods/services for it in return."

Current Crowdfunding Landscape

Just as the women's entrepreneurial ecosystem is continuing to evolve despite uncertainties, so is crowdfunding. These dual evolutions not only allow us to live through disruption, but also to become influencers by shaping the future of both spaces. (More on shaping the future of the women's entrepreneurial ecosystem can be found in Chapter Two.)

A Proliferation of Platforms

Sometimes it seems as if new crowdfunding platforms are being launched by the minute. Innovative entrepreneurs are interested in developing the next big crowdfunding site, no doubt prompted by some early crowdfunding successes, such as:

- Mercury One's 2012 disaster relief effort raised more than two-and-a-half million dollars on Fundly.

Two Kickstarter Success Stories

TouchFire

In fewer than six years, Kickstarter has accounted for more than 57,000 successfully funded projects and attracted more than 5.7 million "investors" collectively contributing more than one billion dollars. Initial fund-raising through these kinds of reward-based crowdfunding platforms helps start-ups materialize and bring their products to market. TouchFire, which offers a keyboard for the iPad, credits much of its initial success to the reward-based crowdfunding model. The company says on its website, "TouchFire started out as a Kickstarter project... TouchFire ended up raising over $200,000 and selling out its entire first production run to Kickstarter backers."

Pono

Another company, Pono, a portable digital media player and music download service for high-quality audio, raised more than six million dollars in investment commitments as of March 2015—nearly seven and a half times its initial $800,000 goal. The company attributes this to an approach that is directly in line with crowdfunding. Pono is now on Crowdfunder, an equity-based crowdfunding site.[71] Chance Barnett, founder of Crowdfunder, comments, "In their Kickstarter campaign, [Pono] did a fantastic job of putting info out about the player and engaging everyday with people as well as with music legends and celebrities to talk about and experience the device."

---

71   http://techli.com/2014/09/is-equity-based-crowdfunding
-right-for-your-startup/#.

- Using Share.Habitat, powered by Fundly, Habitat for Humanity organizers have raised more than $5 million plus to date.[72]

- The COOLEST COOLER campaign on Kickstarter raised more than thirteen million dollars[73] (far exceeding the initial goal of fifty thousand).

- The largest alternative lending platform, LendingClub, which has provided more than six billion dollars of low-interest loans to business-owners, went public late in 2014.[74]

There are more than 200 crowdfunding platforms in the US and 1,250 globally as of 2014.[75] These numbers are increasing, as are the types of crowdfunding—a natural phenomenon during a period of disruptive growth. Many players in the industry—entrepreneurs, investors, and the community of supporters—are rightly excited about the crowdfunding revolution.[76] Others have reservations and

---

72   http://www.habitat.org/wb/news/sharehabitat

73   Key to Crowdfunding: 10 tips for a successful launch: http://www.abcactionnews.com/news/national/key-to-crowdfunding-10-tips-for-a-successful-launch

74   Google partners with Lending Club for loans http://www.sfgate.com/business/bottomline/article/Google-partners-with-Lending-Club-for-loans-6018644.php

75   Massolution Posts Research Findings: Crowdfunding Market Grows 167% in 2014, Crowdfunding Platforms Raise $16.2 Billion: http://www.crowdfundinsider.com/2015/03/65302-massolution-posts-research-findings-crowdfunding-market-grows-167-in-2014-crowdfunding-platforms-raise-16-2-billion/

76   Crowdfunding is the next big thing: http://www.examiner.com/article/crowdfunding-is-the-next-big-thing

are cautiously waiting for the dust to settle. The remaining folks are diligently mapping a course of action to take once all the moving pieces have stabilized.

While all types of crowdfunding are still evolving, equity-based crowdfunding is in its earliest stages. Portfolia founder Trish Costello says, "Platforms like Portfolia, Angel List, and others operate as either angel groups, VC funds, or broker/dealers to provide a global angel platform that breaks down many of the traditional barriers in angel investing, such as geographic barriers, financial requirements, specialization, and administrative expenses, so that entrepreneurs and investors can make a good match." This is another reason for the crowdfunding momentum: the possibilities are endless for what this new platform will enable.

Trish considers Portfolia an accredited investing platform, rather than a crowdfunding platform, since Portfolia has opted to accept investments only from those who meet accreditation guidelines. "To me, the more important thing is that Portfolia is 90 percent women and every other equity investing platform is the mirror opposite, with 90 percent men," Trish says. "You also need to understand that crowdfunding is a catchall phrase and there is very little similarity between Indiegogo/Kickstarter, or GoFundMe, or Lender's Club, or Realty Mogul and an equity platform. They are all called crowdfunding and they are all very different."

Although Trish does not consider Portfolia a crowdfunding platform currently, according to the definition provided in this chapter—or even according to a future definition that may evolve—I identify Portfolia as a future crowdfunding play.

Crowdfunding is gaining traction across various industries, which have adopted it as either a mechanism to generate specific content or ideas from their communities, typically referred to as *crowdsourcing*, or as a tool to raise funds, *crowdfunding*. However, given that crowdfunding, especially equity-based, is in its infancy, many aspects of the practice need to be fleshed out, piloted, iterated, normalized, and mastered. And, finally, supporting laws and regulations must be finalized.

Regulations Affecting Crowdfunding

Some legislation currently exists related to equity-based crowdfunding. This section provides a brief synopsis of current regulations to give angel investors an overview of what is happening with such equity-based crowdfunding platforms. Appendix A provides a more comprehensive look at these regulations.

In 2012, President Barack Obama signed the Jumpstart Our Business Startups (JOBS) Act to encourage funding of small businesses in the US by easing securities regulations.[77] This led to requiring the SEC to write rules and conduct studies around new business ventures' capital formation, registration, and disclosure requirements.[78]

Some of these regulations were enacted immediately on passage of the JOBS Act, but others, especially the ones that relate to crowdfunding have been implemented more slowly. As of March 2015, SEC regulations under Title IV of the JOBS Act of 2012 now permit equity-based

---

77   www.sec.gov/spotlight/jobs-act.shtml

78   Jumpstart Our Business Startups (JOBS) Act https://www.sec .gov/spotlight/jobs-act.shtml

crowdfunding by both accredited and nonaccredited investors. The approval of Regulation A+ is a major break-through in the crowdfunding industry as it allows start-ups and small businesses to raise from accredited investors and the general public up to a maximum of fifty million dollars through crowdfunding.[79]

The JOBS Act consists of seven titles,[80] briefly described below in relationship to their impact on crowdfunding. Titles II, III, and IV are most applicable to crowdfunding. (For more details, see Appendix A.)

The SEC worked hard over the past few years with various pioneers of the crowdfunding industry, both sea-soned and new investors who have an interest in getting this new instrument off the ground, to implement regula-tions that foster and at the same time protect the different players in crowdfunding. As far as investor protection goes, the newly approved Regulation A+ rules allow investors to only invest 10 percent of their additional net worth or annual income in securities.[81]

To keep up to date on the progress and changes to these regulations, visit the SEC website, www.sec.gov/news.

---

79 Crowdfunding Industry Set to Explode as SEC Approves Regulation A+: http://www.huffingtonpost.com/david-drake /crowdfunding-industry-set_b_6953600.html

80 Testimony on JOBS Act Implementation Update http://www .sec.gov/News/Testimony/Detail/Testimony/1365171515996#.U _UzkYBdWLE

81 Crowdfunding Industry Set to Explode as SEC Approves Regulation A+: http://www.huffingtonpost.com/david-drake /crowdfunding-industry-set_b_6953600.html

The Pros of Crowdfunding

Though quite different from the angel investing process, crowdfunding can provide a good entry point into the world of investing. Some of the advantages of equity-based crowdfunding include

- Individual investment amounts can be significantly lower (as little as $5,000 for some platforms such as DreamFunded).

- The crowdfunding platforms often have already vetted and curated the deal flow.

- Crowdfunding's democratization and transparency mean that investors can see, track, and follow other investors who already have a track record of success both on and off crowdfunding platforms.

While these advantages don't make equity-based crowdfunding risk free, its risk is lower relative to other types of investing and it offers a less daunting way to get into the game of early-stage high-risk investing.

Still, there is some controversy in the angel investing community about the use of equity-based crowdfunding. More sophisticated angel investors such as Una Ryan, who invests in biotechnology companies, expressed opposition to crowdfunding as an investment tool because of its current "wild west" status. Investors like Ryan typically invest in capital-intensive technology sectors and thus hesitate to engage with as-yet-unproven tools such as crowdfunding. On the other hand, Susan Preston, a double bottom-line angel (focused on financial returns as well as social impact), finds crowdfunding an exciting space and tool if used for the right start-up industries. Susan invests for high returns but also for high impact, mostly in clean energy due to her concerns for the planet and its environment.

Good for Both Entrepreneurs and Angel Investors

Angels like Susan Preston (author of Chapter Four, on due diligence and valuation) see the potential of crowdfunding to help both entrepreneurs and angel investors. On the entrepreneur's end, she says, "Crowdfunding can take a vital position before the angel round; it can play as substitute for the friends and family round."

Often, a product at the idea stage will garner a lot of attention and demand; the creator can then gauge demand for the product based on the crowd's reaction and buy-in.[82] Equity-based crowdfunding also helps validate the market and/or product for investors, especially around retail, software, mobile, and similar less capital-intensive start-ups that connect with the crowd, although, Preston adds, crowdfunding remains much less common for more "more capital-intensive or complex technology deals, such as in biotech and clean energy" markets.

Efficiency

Another major advantage of crowdfunding is its overall efficiency in the following areas:

---

82 Alicia Robb, PhD, Senior Fellow, Kauffman Foundation — Seeding Ventures: A US Perspective, 2014

1. **Deal sourcing:** crowdfunding enables access to an alternative and larger pool of deals that have already been vetted and curated for success, to which angel investors might not otherwise have had access.

2. **Following and tracking:** companies are visible to potential investors; investors can follow and track companies without a commitment to invest, enabling investment when the angel feels ready. Potential investors also can follow and track lead investors and get on syndications, which is the ability to co-invest with other notable investors for current and future deals.[83] (See Chapter Three for more on syndications.)

3. **No geographical restrictions:** everyone has the same access to deal flow no matter where they live.

4. **Streamlined due diligence:** companies seeking crowdfunding investments provide materials via the platform. This consistent and accessible set of information saves potential investors time, since they don't have to research and chase down material on their own.

5. **An opportunity for market and product validation.** Angel investors often look to the success or failure of a crowdfunding campaign as input into their decision-making about potential investments. According to a 2013 article in *California Magazine*, "Angels are excited about crowdfunding because they see it as a due diligence tool. They can say to a prospect,

83 What is a syndicate: https://angel.co/help/syndicates#what -is-a-syndicate

'Let's see how you sell and market—let's see if people like your product or service. Raise $100,000 through crowdfunding, and we will give you $200,000.'"[84]

Remember, however, that crowdfunding is not an appropriate fund-raising solution in all cases. Some great products, solutions, or business ideas will not entirely succeed on crowdfunding platforms alone due to regulations, especially if they are capital intensive (over fifty million dollars in funding on crowdfunding alone).

The Cons of Crowdfunding

One of crowdfunding's greatest advantages—that it levels the playing field for entrepreneurs and funders and offers a relatively low entry bar—also can be one of its biggest drawbacks. It's precisely this lack of gatekeepers that makes it challenging for less experienced entrepreneurs and funders who may be excited by the great number of potential backers and investments available. After all, not all start-ups that made it to the crowdfunding stage are promising and not all backers an entrepreneur finds on crowdfunding will be good investors.

Smaller Stake in the Venture

Although one of the advantages of crowdfunding is that small amounts of capital can be raised from a large pool

84 Crowded Field: How crowdfunding is changing the investment world: http://alumni.berkeley.edu/california-magazine /just-in/2013-10-27/crowded-field-how-crowdfunding-changing -investment-world

of people, that small amount of capital invested by each funder will typically represent a small percentage ownership in the company invested. When an investor has less skin in the game, she will have less to lose. The investor will probably spend less time and effort trying to add value to the company invested and tend to follow the spray-and-pray approach—investing in a large number of ventures and hoping that one pays off.

Limited Due Diligence

This may mean that potential crowdfunding investors are limited when taking another crucial investing step: due diligence. Susan Preston advises investors to stay objective in their due diligence process. "People often fall in love with the technology and fail to properly analyze the market—how big is it and how accessible, as well as the return potential—can you make a 10X to 20X return?"

Catherine Chiu of Berkeley Angels,[85] an experienced angel investor, dedicates at least thirty hours of due diligence to each company she investigates and feels that even that sometimes is not enough. Of those thirty hours, she might spend five hours simply listening to and working with the entrepreneur on his or her pitch. This may seem like a long time for this activity, but according to Catherine, it's time well spent. By engaging directly with the entrepreneur, an angel can find out how coachable the founder is and if he or she can learn quickly. The rest of the due diligence process involves reviewing financials

---

85 Interviewee: Catherine Chiu, Co-President and chair of the Selection Committee at Berkeley Angels Network

(another good way to validate that the strategy and plans are being reflected in the actual financial road map), checking customer references, negotiating the term sheet, coordinating the syndication with other angels and angel groups planning to co-invest in the round, and drilling the entrepreneurs with additional questions that are key to assessing the risks versus the potential for success.

In some cases, angel investors may shorten the time needed to conduct due diligence by vetting the experience of other angels and checking to see what diligence work has been done. In this case, Catherine Chiu says, she might spend a total of ten to fifteen hours on the process, which would include listening to the pitch, engaging with the entrepreneur, reviewing documents and terms, dialoguing with syndication leader, and asking a few questions of her own. As appropriate, she would dig into particular areas where she feels more work is needed.

Crowdfunding does not offer the opportunity for this lengthy but thorough due diligence process.

According to a *Slate* article, "From an investor's perspective, crowdfunding operates most similarly to angel investment. But most crowdfunding investors won't be able to act like successful angel investors." The article goes on to quote Professor Michael Dorff of Southwestern Law School: "'Successful angel investors invest in industries they know well, do a lot of due diligence, spend time mentoring the companies they invest in, and diversify their investments,' says Dorff. 'And still, the majority of their investments fail completely.' Angel investors only earn a profit because a small percentage of successful companies—about 10 percent, Dorff estimates—make them enough money to offset their other losses."[86]

Crowdfunding may provide a more streamlined process for due diligence as most investors are looking at the same information and probably asking similar questions. However, the due diligence that is available today on crowdfunding platforms is quite limited and almost non-existent compared to what angel investors go through, with the exception of the diligence done by the crowdfunding sites themselves. Given the level of focus and meticulousness required for a thorough analysis, crowdfunding is a long way from being able to support investors and backers in their due diligence process in a manner as comprehensive and robust manner as that conducted by angel investors.

Why We Should Embrace Crowdfunding

I strongly believe crowdfunding is here to stay. Investors are excited about it; the masses want to learn more and get on the bandwagon; crowdfunding investments are happening; and new market entrants believe they can create better crowdfunding platforms, with new services emerging from these innovations. Once a robust regulatory framework is in place, we will have a solid foundation to make equity-based crowdfunding beneficial for everyone in the entrepreneurial eco-system: new early stage businesses, early stage equity investors like angels, and entrepreneurs. My personal

---

86 Kickstarter, but With Stock http://www.slate.com/articles
/business/moneybox/2014/06/sec_and_equity_crowdfunding
_it_s_a_disaster_waiting_to_happen.html

take on crowdfunding is that we should embrace this new kid on the block, learn its potential, and be able to exercise it. One caveat, though is that if we think about all-around access to funding, perhaps crowdfunding—whether donation-based or equity—isn't yet truly democratizing the process. There is still a significant percentage of the population that is unbanked or underbanked[87] and that may not have access to online tools or knowledge to get into crowdfunding. Until we reach a normalized state in crowdfunding, women, crowdfunding platforms and the overall ecosystem players will still have a lot of work to do.

Next Steps for Me—and for You

For me, crowdfunding offered a means to do more to serve underserved audiences, who may not have access to the typical mechanisms for raising capital. Equity-based crowdfunding is an exciting way to expand the definition of fund-raising. My work at Manos Accelerator has been about building an ecosystem of innovation and high-tech entrepreneurship for Latino entrepreneurs in the US. Through my work with SV Links, I hope to build a bridge between Latin America and Silicon Valley innovation and investing ecosystems. I continue to serve the women's entrepreneurial ecosystem through Wingpact. I am excited about the impact crowdfunding can have in all of these areas because it can help empower underserved

---

87 According to the Federal Reserve's 2015 report on consumers and mobile financial services, "The share of consumers who are unbanked is 13 percent, and the share who are underbanked is 14 percent."

communities and make a difference in a meaning-ful way. And as a Kauffman Fellow Class 20,[88] I look forward to expanding my understanding of how funders (venture capitalists and limited partners) also can benefit from crowdfunding.

For an entrepreneur, equity-based crowdfunding may be a natural next step after a successful reward-based crowdfunding campaign, as was the case with Pono, which started on Kickstarter and moved to the equity-based platform Crowdfunder. Individuals looking to invest and diversify their portfolios also are looking to equity-based crowdfunding platforms for the next step in deal sourcing. And new angel investors who used reward-based crowdfunding to become company stakeholders in a relatively low-risk way may be ready to consider equity-based crowd-funding as their next step for equity or ownership in the company.

Money is not the answer to all things, but some-times it is the one element that can make the difference between a thriving start-up and one that's destined to fail. That initial funding push not only makes a busi-ness financially feasible, but it also gives founders the confidence to keep going. And, says Wingee Sin, "For angel investors, equity- or debt-based crowdfunding platforms can be an additional source for deal flow. This can help facilitate the diversification that is much needed in early-stage investing, which is often high risk." (See Chapter Three for more on the importance of diversification.)

---

88   http://www.td.com/document/PDF/economics/special /Crowdfunding.pdf

As suggested in the TD Economics 2014 report on crowdfunding,[89] the best practices framework includes education as one of the key pillars for success, along with regulation and research. Investing in general, whether through crowdfunding or angel investing, is risky and the best way to mitigate those risks is by acquiring knowledge through education and training.

Your next step might be to get involved with the various types of crowdfunding tools, perhaps starting with donation- and reward-based platforms, before moving on to equity-based crowdfunding. (See Appendix B for a listing of some of the currently popular equity-based crowdfunding sites.) When you are ready, you can further your learning by investigating the angel investing training programs offered by the groups such as 37 Angels, Pipeline Angels, Manos Angel Bootcamp, and SV Links Investor Seminar, among others. These can help you demystify and gain knowledge on the end-to-end process of angel investing, theory, tools, and the application of angel investing concepts and processes. Not only are these programs a good resource for those seriously considering angel investing, but they also are a great way to connect with like-minded individuals who want to make an impact in the world of entrepreneurship—like the authors of this book did.

I hope you'll take it upon yourself to participate in the emerging and disruptive funding technique of crowdfunding, to learn and understand how to get into the game by learning about your risk threshold levels, by gaining access to start-ups companies through investments, and also to their backers, entrepreneurs behind the product or

---

89 http://www.td.com/document/PDF/economics/special /Crowdfunding.pdf

company, and fellow new angel investors or seasoned investors who are looking for additional ways to get ahead in the deal sourcing game.

Of course, the ideas in this chapter are not intended to be financial advice, but rather encouragement to explore your comfort with various levels of risk through the new and innovative tool of crowdfunding. Your actions at first are not necessarily about getting it right, but rather about allowing yourself to explore the world of investing.

At its most basic, crowdfunding is about people funding people. Contribution is an amazing act and we are all in a position to do it—especially if we expand the definition of contribution to encompass more than financing. We simply need to find out what each of us can contribute and how. We are in the business of helping create more women angel investors who will then fund more women entrepreneurs. I hope you'll consider where you fit in to that picture.

PART II:
Women's Stories and Voices from the Leading Edge of Angel Investing

The following chapters look at how three women's life experiences—all vastly different and yet connected by common threads—prepared them to become angel investors.

Chapter Seven

Women in Transition

by Karen Bairley Kruger

"There is no tool for development more effective than the empowerment of women." —Kofi Annan

The ending of a marriage requires an acceptance of change and a newfound intimacy with loss. It means leaving everything familiar and stepping into complete darkness, as if boarding an unstable spaceship headed to an unknown universe. When my marriage ended, I did everything I could to remain grounded and strong, even while knowing nothing about where I was destined to go or how I would land. I had loved my ex-husband but our marriage hadn't worked; it was now in the past. Over. The present was a pendulum swinging between grief and optimism and the future was intangible and ambiguous. I had no choice but to move forward—no matter how big the lump in my throat. Yet somewhere deep inside I knew this would be one of the most transformative and empowering journeys I had ever begun.

Finding Riches and Defining Success

After graduate school and before marriage, I made a modest salary as a public school counselor. I was always conscious of the vast economic inequities among students and families. There were years when I worked primarily with teens who were falling through the cracks: victims of abuse, homeless families, and children from houses with neither electricity nor phones. I cared deeply about these students, carried their challenges with me, and felt that helping them in the smallest ways was the reward of my job. I found riches in the work I was doing and with each positive step these students made. I have always defined success by whether I am making a difference in the lives of others, no matter how small. Success means discovering a purpose, dedicating oneself to its pursuit, and mobilizing oneself and others in this pursuit to create positive social impact (more on this later).

Shhh... Money

I stopped working in the fall of 2003 when my husband and I were expecting our first child. I eagerly anticipated becoming a full-time mother. At this point, I turned 100 percent of our financial management over to my husband and focused entirely on the needs of our baby.

My husband and I rarely discussed money. He worked in a lucrative industry, though his role was on the creative side and he had little involvement with deal-making and profits. We exchanged a few words of acknowledgment whenever he was contracted for a new project. Rarely, however, did we talk about the compensation or how we would spend, save, or invest the money.

Because my husband made significantly more than I did, I followed his lead and agreed to his managing our finances. I deferred to him because something felt wrong to me about acknowledging our ample resources. My husband and I were raised in modest homes surrounded by middle-class peers, but as adults, we tried to avoid identifying as wealthy. Ignoring the topic of money seemed to help us pretend we weren't really wealthy, which was somehow easier to accept than the alternative. Our poor communication habits compounded our discomfort about money. Though I believed most couples discussed money, I remained in the dark. I had no sense of ownership or control over our finances. We lived for years with this over-privileged elephant in the room.

It turns out I was far from alone. San Francisco-based marriage and family therapist Maia Taub holds workshops for individuals and couples designed to break taboos around financial issues and the topic of money. The workshops provide an opportunity for clients to share thoughts and feelings around money in a confidential and non-judgmental space. Her goal is for couples to "get very clear about what they want and what is standing in their way. We work with feelings of powerlessness and implement practices to create the relationship with money that they desire." These issues include everything from experiencing a lack of financial control within a relationship to uncertainty about how best to use financial resources to make a positive difference in the world. "I have yet to meet anyone who does not have [some] issues with money," Taub says.

Kathleen Burns Kingsbury, author of *How to Give Financial Advice to Women* and *How to Give Financial Advice to Couples*, believes that taboos around money are "long-standing and destructive." Silence around money, she says, leads 70 percent of families to fail to pass down wealth; contributes to marital problems that can end in divorce when issues aren't addressed; and makes it difficult for parents to raise children who are financially fit. (For more on this topic, visit Kingsbury's website, kbkwealthconnection.com, which features a blog on the psychology of money.)

Kingsbury encourages women and couples to identify their "money mindset" to understand how each one thinks and feels about money and to share these beliefs openly with one another. "Because we don't have practice talking about money and have so many mixed emotions about it, these conversations can initially be difficult." A financial therapist, a life or money coach, or a counselor can help. Kingsbury says that "one of the best things I have done for myself is understand where my ambivalence around money stems from and then address that head on."

Despite the money taboos that had existed within my marriage, I was determined to confront them post-divorce and embrace the crash course in finances that lay ahead.

Personal and Professional Empowerment

A few years after my divorce, I bought a home in San Francisco and began managing a rental property on the East Coast, which became my main source of income. While the relative financial stability was comforting, I found myself lacking a sense of fulfillment. I wanted to continue the positive expansion I'd been experiencing—both personally and professionally.

I considered returning to adolescent counseling, though like most professions, it's not easy returning to work after a ten-year employment gap. I no longer had current references, and very few schools were hiring even if I had had them. This proved to be quite a wake-up call, as I'd always imagined being able to return to work when I was ready. I had never considered how challenging it could be returning to a professional setting after having taken so many years off to raise children. How did I not realize just *how difficult* this could be? All the years nurturing my children and volunteering time at their schools had been exceptionally worthwhile and rewarding, yet proved to be a deterrent in returning to the workforce. I truly had not been aware of the stigmas and challenges associated with resumes that have lapses due to full-time parenting. Although I remained confident that I could overcome these challenges, I felt still defeated and resentful toward society for not protecting the rights of parents who choose to stay home with their children in the early years. My advice to parents choosing to leave the workforce to stay home with their children? Keep a tiny crack in the professional door open, somehow, so the transition back is much easier if and when the time comes to return.

As I began to research new career paths and continued the process of self-rediscovery that divorce often leads to, I realized my professional interests were now very much aligned with women and their ambitions. The thought of helping other women recognize and give voice to their unspoken needs and desires ignited a passion in me. How could I support women through major life transitions? How could I help them live more authentically and take more risks, both personally and professionally? How could I encourage women to examine and redirect their financial resources in ways that could *empower* both themselves and others? These questions weighed on me as I sought a new direction.

Discovering Mission-Aligned Investing

"When we invest in women and girls, we are investing in the people who invest in everyone else."

—Melinda Gates

In the fall of 2013, I began Pipeline Angels, an accelerated angel investing training program for women (see Chapter Two for more on Pipeline Angels). Pipeline Angels fell into my lap with fortuitous timing. I was committed to empowering other women; I had financial resources I had never before "owned"; and my heart had always sought out meaningful social causes. The fellowship was a catalyst to more narrowly define and actualize my professional and personal goals, while giving me access to a network of brilliant, talented, and inspiring like-minded women.

Working with women in an environment created specifically to support female entrepreneurs was transformative. It was during this time that I came to truly understand the gender imbalance among funded entrepreneurs and the statistics that reveal how much more difficult it is for women to secure investments. I had always been aware of glass ceiling struggles but had never heard such shocking personal stories or seen such numbers of professional setbacks due to simply being female. It was truly a privilege to hear business pitches from women entrepreneurs and know that I could play a role in the realization of their ideas and innovations. It was a sense of fulfillment that I had been seeking: I was an angel investor! And the experience was made even greater by the women I met along the way, with whom I continue to share ambitions, ideas, and the mission of making an impact.

A year after the fellowship, I had made two angel investments, understood the importance of combining resources with values, and had seen firsthand the mobilization that results from value-aligned financial choices. Whether or not the companies in which I invested scale and become profitable, more women have come to the table and more women have been seen, heard, and funded. This in itself has made the investments worthwhile.

Social Impact and Social Entrepreneurship

Social impact can be defined as "the effect of an activity on the social fabric of the community and well-being of individuals and families" (Businessdictionary.com). The common thread among the myriad definitions of social impact is that one's actions can make a positive difference in the world. This is exactly the approach I had always taken in my work and personal life.

A social entrepreneur is born when you combine a desire to make a social impact with the ambition to start a new business. It is "a person who pursues an innovative idea with the potential to solve a community problem."[1]

As I entered the world of angel investing, I discovered an abundance of women—both investors and entrepreneurs—who sought the same sense of personal, professional, and financial fulfillment that I did. Many also were mothers attempting to manage their professional lives

---

1 Investopedia.com

Spotlight: The Inspirational Woman Project

Bri Seeley, fashion designer and founder of the Inspirational Woman Project, is an entrepreneur dedicated to helping women discover their best selves and live a life of purpose. She's motivated by seeing women inspired within their womanhood, their professional passions, and their personal lives. After being unfilled in a nine-to-five job for many years, Bri decided to launch a 31-day blog series with three questions around what it means to be a woman and why it's so great to be a woman. Her writing was met with so much interest and response that she was soon invited to blog for the Huffington Post. Within months, Bri left her day job, continued blogging, and launched the Inspirational Woman Project, a coffee-table book consisting of 99 interviews with women from around the world. The project took off rapidly and surpassed its crowdfunding goal on Kickstarter. Bri's diverse collection of personal interviews has led to speaking engagements and book signings around the country, as well as Inspirational Woman Workshops, which began in 2015.

Bri is an example of the power generated by women believing in themselves, collaborating, and supporting each other. She realized from the 99 interviews that "most women don't believe in their own power. They don't think that their contributions to the world are inspirational." Her advice to women is to "figure out what's inspirational about you, own it, and share it with the world!" She encourages women to move past cultural pressure and the media's negative messages to "tap into the expansion that women can create together. One woman is powerful in and of herself but the power of combining several women together is unstoppable!"

alongside their personal and family priorities. Most striking to me was that so many women were also determined to make an impact in the world. Their stories resonated loudly. I realized the world needed to hear about these common motivations bringing women into the world of entrepreneurship.

The stories that follow represent only a few examples of successful female social entrepreneurs I had the pleasure of speaking with about their experiences getting their companies off the ground. But they represent a much wider pool of women working in countless ways to create social impact.

Ennaid Therapeutics: Giving Up is Not an Option

Darnisha Grant Harrison, the founder and CEO of Ennaid Therapeutics, began her entrepreneurial journey in 2012 by seeking funding from family and friends. To complete her seed round of funding, she sold her personal assets, including her home and car, and plowed the proceeds into her start-up. She viewed this bootstrapping as a testament to her dedication to and confidence in her mission.

Darnisha's more than two decades of work in the field of life sciences as a microbiologist and chemist and her nineteen years of experience in the pharmaceutical industry gave her the foundation to launch Ennaid Therapeutics, a biopharmaceutical company developing cures for mosquito-borne infectious diseases for nearly one billion people worldwide. The company targets ten diseases, including West Nile Virus, yellow fever, and all four strains of dengue virus, which is the world's fastest-growing pandemic. Ennaid Therapeutics is developing a technology that inhibits these viruses by 99 percent and is expected to be on the market around 2020.

"Selling my home was acid proof that I wholeheartedly believed in Ennaid Therapeutics," Darnisha says, and adds that she was then able to move on to the next round of funding through seeking grants and venture capital funds.

Being female and African-American while embarking on the entrepreneurial road has not been without its challenges. However, Darnisha believes that the biggest obstacle of all is not fully believing in oneself. "For females and minorities, it's often the fact that we don't represent the majority of founders [and] CEOs out there, [as] most are white males. That in itself can sometimes be immensely intimidating. My advice [is] to continue giving 100 percent to your venture while maintaining a laser focus on your desired end result, no matter what things look like around you and no matter how many 'nos' you may hear. And always continue moving forward with a settled knowing in the very seat of your soul that giving up is not an option."

PhilanTech: Know What You Know, and What You Don't

Dahna Goldstein is the founder and CEO of PhilanTech, an online platform enabling nonprofit grant seekers and grant funders to connect and streamline their work together. PhilanTech contributes to the social good by enabling social sector organizations to facilitate and expedite important connections between grant makers and grantees.

Her advice to tech entrepreneurs is to "ensure that what you are creating is meeting a need—that it's a solution to a problem that people, businesses, organizations, [or] the target market feels." She emphasizes that people must be willing and able to pay for the product or service, and understand the purpose behind what it offers.

"Know how you are going to get your first customer, then your next ten and your next hundred. If you are raising money, show your potential investors the need you are addressing, your plan for customer acquisition, and how you'll eventually return their investment." She encourages entrepreneurs to recognize and acknowledge what they know and don't know. "You are an expert in your business—and you should be. But you'll need other experts, including your investors. Knowing where your knowledge and experience will be bolstered by others is incredibly helpful."

Kuli Kuli:[2] They'll Never Say Yes if You Don't Ask

Lisa Curtis, founder and CEO of Kuli Kuli, came up with her business idea after serving as a volunteer in the Peace Corps in Niger, Africa. There she was introduced to a hearty, drought-resistant, nutrient-dense plant called *Moringa oleifera*, long used to fight and prevent malnutrition in developing countries. After realizing the potential of this superfood, Lisa brought it to the United States and now sells it in powder form as well as in three varieties of nutrition bars. Kuli Kuli products can be found in more than 300 stores in the US, including Whole Foods, Fred Meyer, and Raley's. The company continues to support women farming cooperatives in West Africa by sourcing directly from women farmers and paying an average of 30 percent above the market price for Moringa. Kuli Kuli is an example of a successful woman-founded,

---

2   Full disclosure: Three authors of this book made an early-stage angel investment in Kuli Kuli.

mission-driven business that is both rapidly scaling and making a difference.

This is not to say Lisa's path was always smooth. Looking back on the obstacles she encountered as a young entrepreneur in the beginning stages of business, Lisa mentioned multiple challenges around securing funding as one of very few females seeking venture capital. The sexism she encountered on the part of male venture capitalists was both overt and discouraging. After winning one pitch event in San Francisco, Lisa was told by an organizer that she only won "because I am a 'total babe' [and] not because my business or pitch had any merit." At the same event, a judge from the investor panel told Lisa he thought her winning was a mistake. "It was horrible and truly eye-opening," she said. "It makes me so glad that more women are becoming angel investors."

Lisa's advice to other female entrepreneurs: "Develop very thick skin and keep putting yourself out there. The worst that anyone can say is no but they'll never say yes if you don't ask."

SOLO Eyewear: Capable of Amazing Things

Every time SOLO Eyewear sells a pair of its handcrafted, recycled bamboo sunglasses, the company provides a pair of prescription glasses or helps fund eye surgery for a person in need.

SOLO Eyewear founder Jenny Amaraneni conceived of the idea for this mission-driven company during the months she spent researching eye care around the world for a graduate school project. She recruited an ambitious co-worker, Dana Holliday, as a partner. Together they developed a product, launched a website, and began selling within months. SOLO Eyewear has since funded eye care for nearly 10,000 people in nineteen countries.

The obstacle Jenny remembers most vividly when getting SOLO off the ground was entering a male-dominated business culture. "It's easy to second guess yourself or feel undermined in conversations about your idea," she says. She emphasizes the importance of believing in oneself and remaining determined. "We are all capable of accomplishing amazing things."

KangaDo: Believe in Yourself and Be Headstrong

Sara Schaer could have been a customer for the business she founded. She built KangaDo, an app for busy parents that offers services such as on-demand rides and childcare, while raising two children.

Sara's advice to women entrepreneurs whose families, friends, or investors question their ability to juggle both roles is to have answers at the ready "so that you can continue to project confidence and don't get caught off guard. Believe in yourself and be headstrong." Schaer was proud to hear that her young son was running an imaginary business on his school playground and viewed his ambition as a validation of her own work. "Some might think that my kids would complain about my workload. However, it has proven to be a source of inspiration for them."

O-Venture: Don't Let Obstacles Be Deterrents

Janie Cooke and Caroline Nix, founders of O-Venture, are examples of how motherhood does not have to be a deterrent to starting one's own business. O-Venture makes stylish, fun, oversized key rings and accessories. (One of their most popular items is humorously called "the Big O.") As busy mothers, Janie and Caroline were confident that their product would appeal to women everywhere who never wanted to misplace their keys again. O-Venture has been featured in many magazines, including *Elle* and *Esquire*. It also won the Spanx Leg Up award, landing a promotional spot in the popular Spanx catalog, and was selected as one of "Oprah's Favorite Things 2014."

While on the road to profitability, Janie and Caroline became aware of the obstacles female entrepreneurs face when launching a business. Women have far fewer resources at their disposal than men. This includes everything from securing funding and accessing professional networks to the fact that women are more often the primary family caregivers, having to juggle parenthood while simultaneously nurturing career aspirations. Women don't "have the long and uninterrupted work history of their male counterparts," they say. But they do have "the unique blend of creativity, smarts, and empathy" needed to run a successful business.

Janie and Caroline's advice to female entrepreneurs: stay the course and don't let obstacles be deterrents. Seek wisdom from other women in business, ask questions, and never discount another's potential to be a helpful source of information. "Be confident and realize that one conversation could lead to a huge opportunity," they say. "Women helping other women is the best way to pay it forward and, in our mind[s], the best investment in our future."

Mom-preneurs and Finding the Elusive "Balance"

Some women who start—or think about starting—their own ventures are also mothers, sometimes of young children. For many mothers, the thought of starting a business is intimidating and seems nearly impossible. How could we juggle even more responsibilities than we already have at home? Marla Tabaka (inc.com), a small-business advisor with more than twenty-five years of experience in corporate and start-up ventures, says, "Moms don't have eight or more consecutive hours a day to devote to a business. Instead they are filtering through conflicting priorities, enduring constant interruptions, and working to maintain a professional front—all while trying their darnedest to be great moms."

So how can busy moms achieve the necessary balance to succeed at both home life and entrepreneurial life? Maybe the answer is not to seek balance but to allow one's ambitions unfold organically. While a mother might enjoy parenting full-time one year, the following year doesn't have to look the same. As humans, our needs and desires evolve; it is our responsibility as women to tend to these needs and nurture them just as we nurture the needs of our children. The focus in our conversations shouldn't be on how to do it all, but rather on when to do A, B or C. It's taking everything on *simultaneously* that is overwhelming—and often impossible. We should focus instead on setting priorities for each new stage in life, delegating responsibilities and finding help when needed. It is up to us, as individuals, to make sure we attend to our needs, dreams, and desires *along with* those of our families.

Single-mom entrepreneurs have unique challenges, as they may not have the financial resources that joint-income couples or married mom-preneurs have to fall back on. However, there are some upsides to this status as well. Angela Benton, founder and CEO of NewMe, which has raised more than $17 million in venture capital funding for start-ups, says that "being a single mom is not a setback... Being a single mom comes with a wealth of skills that do well in entrepreneurship: multitasking, creativity, managing, operating on a budget, and problem solving. I'd put my money on someone with these skills rather than a new college grad."[3]

Whether single or coupled, raising one child or many, women must remember that their dreams and goals are essential to a happy and fulfilling life. Take one bite at a time, nurture and love your children, but don't forget to feed yourself too. Tending to your needs and desires when time allows will make you a happier mom, and happier moms are better moms. And when the dreaded pressure of "balance" creeps back into your psyche, remember that moving forward might require a bit of temporary *imbalance*. I encourage you to write down your own personal definition of balance and remember that it does *not* have to mean succeeding at everything simultaneously. Your definition is unique to you and you'll achieve balance only if you keep *your* definition front and center as you work toward your goals.

Connecting Entrepreneurs with Angels

The main purpose of this book is not only to encourage women with financial resources to consider funding

---

3 http://www.entrepreneur.com/slideshow/239018

female entrepreneurs, but to encourage female entrepreneurs to *seek out* this funding. From crowdfunding to pitching a business directly to angel groups, do not be discouraged by a lack of funds. Seize every opportunity to get your idea heard, be receptive to feedback, and maintain very thick skin. If *you* truly believe in your product, service or mission, others will too. Do not be afraid to ask for money—ask and ask again! Be comfortable requesting the funds you need because there are investors out there who are searching for determined, impassioned entrepreneurs just like you, who are dedicated and hell-bent on making a difference.

Let's Talk!

While I will always cherish the days of being a new mother and am extremely grateful to have been able to stay home with my kids while they were little, I do wish I had attended more to the financial structure of my family during those early years of motherhood. I could have initiated more conversations with my husband about money; I could have learned more about investing and discussed the topic with like-minded peers; and I could have recognized myself as a more powerful agent of change. In other words, if I had simply felt comfortable talking about money, I could have leveraged my financial agency *beyond* what my husband and I were contributing to our family, charity, and personal causes. Our resources could have been used to *mobilize* others and empower entrepreneurs with brilliant and innovative ideas, specifically those who were committed to making a positive social change.

For entrepreneurs, mom-preneurs, investors, and *all* women, I challenge you to own, acknowledge, and talk about money. But don't talk just to the women in your lives. Talk to the men in your lives and enlist them as allies. Tell men about the obstacles women still face in business today and how *everyone*—from your own family to corporations' bottom lines to the US economy as a whole—benefits from greater gender diversity and hearing more women's voices.

Sonia Oster, founder and CEO of the social learning platform Aprentica, agrees that in order for women to create a better business environment we need to stop talking only amongst ourselves. We need to "explain [to men] the obstacles women face, show men how to better support women in business, and help [them] understand that women are great leaders and an outstanding investment."

Kathleen Burns Kingsbury also suggests that we surround ourselves with empowered, financially astute peers. "Make sure you have a friend or two in your life who sees the value of women being empowered financially and then support each other as you take steps to embrace your financial power."

Anu Bhardwaj, founder of the Women Investing in Women Institute, reiterates that this is a critical time for entrepreneurs to access capital and for more women to fund other women: "We have money; we have power; we need to focus on each other."

What are we waiting for? Let's get talking, shatter money taboos, and maximize our financial agency. While bringing more women to the table, we will each become an integral part of the personal, social, and economic transformations brought about by women investing in women.

Get comfortable with money, and start the conversation!

Chapter Eight

The Matriarch

by Christine Emilie Lim

Having a female role model early on, especially within my family, molded my approach to taking charge of my finances starting in my teenage years. As an angel investor, I have been able to use my skills, learned primarily from my female role model, in communicating with entrepreneurs and negotiating company valuation. My ability to take calculated risks and to communicate and negotiate judiciously— all important assets as an angel investor–reflect the influence of the fiercest woman I know.

As the clock struck noon, a woman glided into our family dining room. She peered through thick brown-rimmed glasses and patted her curly, coiffed, dyed light brown hair with a hand sporting perfectly manicured blood-red nails. She wore her usual sleeveless blouse, maroon with multi-colored flowers, paired with black slacks. Small beads of sweat had started to form on her wrinkled forehead due to the sweltering tropical heat of the Philippines.

"Where is the youngest girl?" she asked. Her commanding voice boomed inside the dining room, which was just big enough to fit a family of seven.

The household helper knocked on one of the upstairs bedroom doors and peered inside. "It is time to eat. Your grandmother is in the dining room now."

I looked up. My eight-year-old self was preoccupied watching my favorite Sunday noontime cartoon show, *Sailormoon*. I knew I had to run downstairs or risk that my grandmother would reprimand me for the second time that day. Earlier that morning, she had delivered her sermon on why I should wake up early and not miss any more 6:30 a.m. church masses. I quickly rolled out from my bed, finger-combed my thick unruly hair, and ran downstairs in my pajamas—leaving *Sailormoon*, a blonde female action hero with two female sidekicks, behind to fend off the bad guys on television.

The smell of pungent garlic and bay leaves from the chicken adobo greeted me as I rushed into the dining room. Glass-fronted cabinets around the walls held antique silverware my grandmother had purchased during her travels overseas. The floral wallpaper complemented the yellow earthy tones of the cabinets and wooden dining table and chairs.

Just like every other Sunday lunch, my grandmother had prepared a full menu aimed at showing off her prowess in entertaining a large group. Our six-foot by four-foot dining table was filled with large plates of vermicelli noodles with vegetables, white rice, *humba* (pork belly), chicken adobo, grilled *bangus* (milkfish), and a pitcher of fresh coconut water from the coconuts that had fallen off the trees in our garden.

Our family of seven was now all in the same room. As I took my grandmother's right hand and bowed my forehead to touch it, a Filipino gesture of respect to elders, I could feel her big dark brown eyes staring at me as if to silently tell me that I should not be late for family meals. Ever. She hurriedly ushered me to wash my hands and take my seat, both of which I did obediently.

These meals would continue in similar fashion for the next six years, and for all of them, I would sit on the dining chair across from the fiercest woman I have ever known: my grandmother, whom I call Ama in Hokkien Chinese. To others, she was known as Doña Conchita, the force behind both running our household and our thirty-plus-year-old family business.

In our dining room, or in any room, in fact, she was the loudest, the most talkative and the most in command. As lunch progressed and the bowl of steaming white rice disappeared, conversations between my grandparents and parents circled around how our family business in agriculture was doing. Did the shipment arrive? How or why are the prices fluctuating? Were any employees leaving or asking for an advance pay? Who do we need to hire? When is the typhoon coming so we can prepare for the worst? Rarely was the discussion about how my siblings and I were doing in school, who was celebrating a special occasion, or what we were going to do during our nearing summer break; those conversations were saved for non-dining hours. I kept quiet throughout the meal and spoke only when asked a question. I couldn't have known it then, but listening to these conversations prepared me for something I would undertake many years in the future. The risk level of projects you support as an angel investor is often high; staying abreast of trends and the current business trends minimizes this risk. Ama's incisive questions helped her do exactly that.

Despite being in deep conversation about business matters, Ama was quick to shift topics to ensure that no one left the table hungry. "Are you full yet?" she asked. I nodded with my mouth full. She was a great cook and had a passion for putting fire in her mouth, literally. Throughout the meal, my Ama reached for a platter of small red chilies freshly picked from our backyard and soaked in vinegar. For her, nothing tasted good without chilies.

Ama's personality was as feisty as the fiery flavors she loved. This was especially evident when she engaged in her side business: trading diamonds. A few hours after lunch that day, the doorbell rang. Ama's friend, whom I guessed was just a few years younger than she, came to our house to show her the latest diamonds and gold jewelry, which she carried in a small pouch.

Diamond trading is a risky business if you are not well trained to quickly detect a fake or determine actual value. As my Ama's friend took a seat on our maroon-colored, paisley-printed family couch, I sat and waited on the lower staircase facing the living room, watching and listening, curious about what the adults were doing. I heard a few "oohs" and "ahs" and even saw a twinkle of light as a gold bangle reflected the sunlight from the window. Ama pulled out her magnifying glass and peered through it like Sherlock Holmes at one of the rocks to check its authenticity. After a few lightning-fast rounds of bargaining, the seller left our house with a check in hand and fewer diamonds in her pouch. Ama was an aggressive negotiator, showing no hint of uncertainty in her voice or actions. She was always in control, especially when it came to business. I was always fascinated by how she maintained full command of any situation without so much as a twitch of her eyebrow.

Business done, Ama called me to start practicing piano. I scrambled up from the hardwood stairs and opened the piano chair to take out my music book, then closed it and sat on the uncomfortable surface. I had less than two weeks to master Beethoven's "Für Elise" for my piano recital so I could graduate to the next level.

Every Friday after school, my Ama, a trained classical pianist, accompanied me to my piano classes and asked my teacher how I was doing. To Ama's disappointment, my teacher always scolded me for not showing enough emotion while playing Beethoven or Mozart—or any classical piano piece, for that matter. For years I had watched Ama play with gusto on our shiny black grand piano, swaying lyrically, keeping both hands in perfect egg-shaped formation while playing staccato notes, and pressing the foot pedal with precision timing. I knew I could never play as well as she did.

My rendering of "Für Elise" was robotic. With my body as stiff as a toothpick, I was able to get through the entire piece without making a mistake thanks to pure memorization and many hours of practicing. I learned early on from my Ama the value of self-discipline that came with committing to an endeavor. Whether I was any good at it is a completely different story, but the ability to maintain commitment to something has served me well.

Though Ama was a strict disciplinarian, she knew how to reward hard work with an approach akin to Pavlov's classical conditioning. After listening for an hour to multiple repetitions of the same sequence of notes, Ama finally brought in a bowl of her special recipe of *binignit*, a thick vegetable coconut soup with saba bananas, sweet potato, taro, and glutinous rice flour balls. The sweet smell of *binignit* brought a smile to my lips, and I immediately relaxed my tensed shoulder muscles. Finally, I was done with piano practice for the day and ready to gobble up Ama's treat.

By 6 p.m., the sun was setting and turning the sky an array of pink and orange. Everyone was already dressed in their best dining attire to attend a family friend's wedding party. Soon after, we were all whisked away to a convention center that doubled as an event space thirty minutes from our home. As expected, the hundreds of onlookers in the ballroom quieted down when my Ama entered dressed in her custom-made, floor-length cream-colored Maria Clara, a traditional gown worn by women in the Philippines. Doña Conchita had arrived.

I observed my Ama countless times at gatherings of family or friends. She was always the social butterfly with her boisterous laughter and endless stories. Her commanding presence was undeniable; her high-pitched voice carried to the end of the room. She was always in her element as she said hello to her acquaintances and kissed her lady friends cheek-to-cheek. She was an extremely opinionated extrovert who could carry a conversation on subjects ranging from family matters to the global economy.

That same year, I started working part-time for our family business. I would wake to the omnipresent forty-degree Celsius heat of another sweltering summer season. In the morning, my job was to count the different types of sacks of rice to ensure that no one had stolen our inventory the night before. At the end of the day, I counted cash on hand before closing the store.

Ama kept a keen eye on me since I had a penchant for frolicking in the middle of the day. I was a curious youngster, after all. She didn't hesitate to admonish me if she caught me goofing around and playing hide-and-seek with one of our employee's children, between towers of rice sacks. Yet Ama was even stricter with our employees. She was quick to correct anyone lazing around or fire someone caught stealing supplies or lying.

Six years later, Ama's health declined. At seventy-six, she struggled with cancer of the bone marrow, a rare disease for someone of Asian/Spanish heritage. Her words slurred. She walked slowly. There were days she couldn't even get up from her bed. Her orchids, left untended, wilted in our garden. The floral wallpaper in our kitchen started peeling.

After struggling for many months, Ama passed away peacefully in her bedroom. I sat on the same wooden staircase where I had sat years earlier listening to her haggle over diamonds and watched the paramedics carry her lifeless body out of our house.

* * *

On a chilly November Monday morning in 2010, I was ushered into a conference room a few minutes after 8 a.m. I was about to embark on another journey as a recent MBA graduate; it was my first day at a new job in Silicon Valley. With only the projector's light casting a glow on everyone's faces, we exchanged polite smiles as I was introduced. I was the only female in a room full of a dozen male senior managers and directors.

I was not perturbed. Because I sat across the dining table from the fiercest woman I have ever known for the first fourteen years of my life, I had learned lessons that I hadn't even realized she was teaching. I was also given the opportunity to work without gender biases at such a young age with my Ama as my supervisor in a country that globally ranks ninth in gender equality.[4]

Ama, the matriarch, was a woman ahead of her time. She had weathered the World War II era in the Philippines to build a fledgling family business and a tight-knit family. She was able to balance her work and personal lives and exert a strong positive influence on others, which is a form of female empowerment. Not only did she teach me the values of obedience, thriftiness, and respect for the elderly, she also showed me early on how to empower myself as a female by taking calculated risks through hard work, self-discipline, and a strong business acumen—all of which drove me to become an angel investor.

---

4   The World Economic Forum's Global Gender Gap Index, 2014.

Chapter Nine

Past, Present, Future: Beads of Our Lives Woven on a Thread of Time

by Jagruti Bhikha

"To call woman the weaker sex is a libel; it is man's injustice to woman. If by strength is meant brute strength, then, indeed, is woman less brute than man. If by strength is meant moral power, then woman is immeasurably man's superior. Has she not greater intuition, is she not more self-sacrificing, has she not greater powers of endurance, has she not greater courage? Without her, man could not be. If nonviolence is the law of our being, the future is with woman. Who can make a more effective appeal to the heart than woman?"

—Mahatma Gandhi

My intention with this chapter is to convince you, as an aspiring woman entrepreneur, innovator, or investor, that inspiration, love, courage, faith, and imagination can make your dreams a reality.

I chose to write this as an inspirational piece because to me it's more vital to find out the *why* behind your dreams than to focus on the *how*. The *how* usually happens as a side benefit of knowing and believing in your *why*. *Why* also inspires us through the times when we doubt ourselves. My fellow authors have given you both *why* and *how* stories; I focus exclusively on the *why*.

As you begin to uncover the *why* that propels you, you can encourage and support others in their journeys. I hope my observations will inspire you to learn from your past while remaining in the present and contemplating your journey into the future, first as a woman and then as an entrepreneur or investor.

The Past: Recognizing Women as the World's Largest Untapped Resource

It was a humid summer evening in 1942. Outside dark clouds were rolling in, as if in preparation to cleanse and renew the earth, just as we renew ourselves with a meal with our loved ones and then rest for the night in our homes. But the streets of Jamnagar, India were not resting that evening. They were silently buzzing. No one had to speak, because you could see it in their faces, read it in their eyes, and feel it in the fire burning in their hearts.

This is the way my favorite story begins, a story my father told often.

Jamnagar was a city of Jains, Hindus, and a small population of Muslims. Despite their differences, they spent that summer evening in 1942 chanting in unison: "Bharat Mata ki Jai Ho!" ("May the victory come to Mother India!") The streets were alive with sights, smells, and sounds of excitement, courage, faith, and belief. My father was among the crowd. The fact that he was there for one of the biggest events in the history of India—if not the world—was a source of great pride for him. His eyes sparkled like the most precious diamonds as he told me the story.

The event was not uncommon; these sorts of events were being held all over India as she was getting ready to free herself from the British Raj. Over the last few centuries India had been under the rule of the British. I had learned from my school history about the many people who sacrificed their lives to free India from the British Raj by participating in fights and protests like the one my father described. However, the words my father spoke felt so powerful and engaging that even the most interesting facts and stories from the school books seemed boring. A light shone in his eyes, as if in telling the story he could transport himself from the present to that day in 1942 and experience the same emotions, energy, and excitement he had felt then. As his biggest admirer, I loved to see that excitement come alive in my father.

I am the youngest of seven siblings. My only brother led the way, followed by my five older sisters and me. Circumstance prevented me from getting to know many of my siblings until after I reached adulthood, but if you asked them, they would probably say that I have always been the different one. I consider myself a product of three key locations: India, America, and my imagination. All three have played a strong part in who I have become.

India: Life in the Chawls

My family took up residence in a lower middle class community in one of the so-called chawls (tenement buildings) of Mumbai. The chawl we lived in was not multi-story, as was typical of those structures. Rather, we lived on the ground level in a space so cramped that the shower was part of the kitchen. We used to have to wait until all the dishes and clothes had been washed before we could take a shower. The community toilets, shared by twenty families, stood at least fifty yards away from the building. Next to the toilets was a well of what we called "municipal water," a single water source used by many people without access to the city lines. We were all supposed to have access to city water, but sometimes, when you turned on the tap, nothing came.

Staples like sugar, flour, and milk were not as available as we wanted them to be. One of my earliest memories is of standing in a line for government goods that we could purchase at a lower cost. Sometimes adults would cut to the front of the line, preventing me from getting what I had come to gather for my family. At seven years old, I could do little to stop them.

The chawls had their share of stories. Mothers worshipping cobras and offering milk, only to see them slither away, ungrateful; ghosts living in the peepal tree (the holiest of trees in Indian culture) in the open field behind the chawl; women committing suicide by jumping in the well from which we and others used to fetch water; child abuse and domestic violence; the celebration of Diwali, Eid, Holi, the Kite Festival, and so on. My early years were painted with all the colors of humanity: ugly and beautiful, sad and happy, loud and quiet, together and alone… all the polarities of life.

At the same time, whenever I stepped into my home, which was probably no more than ten feet by twenty feet with a kitchen and living/bedroom combined, the noises of the outside world were erased and replaced by the voices of my family. Sometimes the voices were kind. Sometimes they were angry. But most times, the intention was clear: to love and protect and provide. At night, we all spread out our blankets and pillows and slept next to each other while my parents made their bed in the kitchen area. There was no air conditioning and no heat. In fact, we didn't even know what those things were.

My parents were not educated at all but they agreed to send my brother (the only son and the oldest of their children) to America for further studies in engineering. They didn't have means to give him anything more than the money for the plane ticket. Many people told my parents that they were making a big mistake to send their only son away to a foreign country. The effects of British governance still lingered; anyone who looked white or seemed to come from a foreign country might be perceived as a threat. I can't imagine what my parents went through to make that decision, which changed my brother's life forever. It was a decision that changed my life, too, as my brother "paid it forward" by supporting me in getting to the United States.

I was only two years old when my brother left for America, where he completed his graduate studies in engineering. My brother made a living as a student and sent some of the funds to my parents. I can only imagine the looks on the faces of those who had criticized my parents for sending away their only son as they saw our life getting better economically.

When I was in 10th standard (the Indian equivalent of the last year of high school in the US), my mother passed away at the young age of fifty-three, followed by my father not long after. In-between their deaths, I managed to find my way to America to live with my brother. That was the second decision that changed my life—and I had nothing to do with making it. Others—specifically my father and my brother—decided that I should go. I am thankful to my father and my brother for having made the decision on my behalf because it changed my life for the better. Still, that's when I realized I was a woman, at least according to the norms of my native culture. I had to get used to other people deciding things for me. I knew they loved me, but that didn't change the fact that as a woman, I had no power.

Thus began my journey, in my mid-teens, from the only world I knew to a completely new world: India to America, east to west.

America: Beginning in the United States

At age sixteen, I started at college at SUNY at Stony Brook. The first semester, you could usually find me walking around observing people, eating french fries, salads, and milkshakes (I am vegetarian), failing classes, and crying myself to sleep almost every night. I was a resident of Long Island, New York, and yet I didn't know English. As someone so used to reading, writing, and creating stories, not being able to communicate was like not being able to breathe. I was away from everything I knew: language, people, culture, tradition, and school.

One day, I was walking around the SUNY campus by myself—a petite girl with a long, oiled braid, a giant winter jacket, and a huge red dot on her forehead—when a few young men started following me. It took me a while to realize that I had become a target for their entertainment.

They started walking closer to me and saying words I didn't understand. I was frightened at first, but then I remembered something I had heard from a friend at my school in India who was always getting into trouble: when in doubt, smile (and do it with grace and kindness). So I made an eye contact and smiled at them.

They replied by pointing at my bindi and calling me "dothead." I kept walking with my head held high and my lips breaking into the occasional unflappable smile. This was enough to drive them away.

When I ran back to my dorm room that day, it was with the knowledge that I had become weak. Until that moment, I hadn't known what it felt like to be weak, to let strangers get in your head and do things to you that you can't get rid of. I had known the power my loved ones held over me—and sometimes they did and said painful things—but to have a stranger hold that power over me was a new feeling. I felt uneasy that day and I walked around campus aimlessly, as if the answer to my question lay in the beautiful branches of the tree or in the ice hiding itself under the cover of freshly fallen snow waiting to surprise me as I slipped and made contact with the hardness underneath.

An answer eventually came, like a whisper breathed in my ear as I walked the lonely, scary path between the main campus and my dorm room. The answer was: if I was going to regain my power, first I had to fit in. I couldn't be who I used to be. I had to get my hair cut, take off my *bindi*, wear western clothes, and start eating meat. I will never forget that day. It was the day I realized that the world is not as it exists in my books or in my heart. Good or bad, fitting in was the answer that came to me then, even though I know

now that is not the answer I would find today.

The streets of Mumbai taught me much—especially how to be a woman who doesn't attract negative attention. The campus of SUNY at Stony Brook taught me that learning to blend in is a huge part of that effort. From that day forward, I was a changed woman, for better or worse.

America: Moves and Transitions

I graduated with a BS degree in electrical engineering and computer science. I accepted my first job at Motorola in Fort Lauderdale. Florida reminded me of Mumbai. I lived there for eleven years. I married and my two beautiful daughters were born there. I can say that this was one of the most beautiful times in my life. My husband and I were very happy being parents. But we were also seeking to advance our careers in technology. So, when California came calling—with hopes of a better career, more money, the opportunity to learn new things, and beautiful weather—we decided to take a chance on starting yet again.   For the first time since I had left India, I made a move that filled me with hope and dreams for a better life for my family.

Years passed. California kept its promise. It gave us more opportunities, better lives and beautiful weather. We planted ourselves. Then another opportunity came calling, this one for my husband, to move to Hong Kong for his job. I was not thrilled with this decision. By that time my daughters were nine and twelve. I had a career that allowed me to raise my daughters while continuing to be part of the tech scene. I would have to change jobs and my daughters would have to change schools. Nonetheless, we decided it was best for the family to be together in Hong Kong rather than having my husband shuttle back and forth. I ended up living in Hong Kong with my family.

It was a bittersweet experience, because that's when my marriage ended. By the time I had picked up the pieces, I realized I had another decision to make: to stay in Hong Kong or move back to California. For the sake of my daughters, I decided to return to California.

For years after returning, I spent sleepless nights worrying. I worried about whether I was capable as a single parent. I worried about losing my job, about someone breaking into the house. Endless "what-ifs" ruled my life for many years. I became bitter, paranoid, unhappy, and resentful, but somehow remained driven to make life better for myself and my children.

The past decade has been about watching my daughters become young adults. My journey as a working single mom in technology led to several career changes, homebuilding projects, and life advancements. My daughters went off to college and I became an empty-nester; one of my daughters graduated and boomeranged home. At the time of this writing, she is building her life working at a start-up. Life can teach you things in the most shocking way. But I should know that. My past is filled with those lessons.

The Imagination: Books and Storytelling

My favorite pastime as a child was reading books. My passion for storytelling was so great that whenever a teacher was absent from school my classmates would insist that I get up in front of the class and tell stories to pass the time. I remember making up stories about ghosts, murders, and animate household objects. I retold historical stories with my own plot twists.

At one point, I had read every single book in my school's library (which was admittedly no bigger than four feet by four feet, just large enough for two people to fit inside at once). The rule was that no one was allowed to borrow more than two books per week, but I bargained with the librarian to allow me a book a day in exchange for my help organizing the library.

The joy of reading has stuck with me—to the point where I often feel like I am more comfortable with books than with people. When I travel to a new city, I always look for bookstores and libraries; they are my most comfortable hangouts. If I am not reading, I am watching people reading—getting lost somewhere without leaving the comfort of their chairs.

I still love to write and create stories, but now my stories are more often than not about how I can make something better—how I can innovate and find new ways to do something, or create things with my imagination, my soul, and my heart aligned. I find moments of joy when nothing is more important than the excitement of executing an idea.

The Present: Worship, Murder, and Knowledge

A few years ago an event that happened to someone I didn't know personally ended up affecting my life deeply. I learned about what happened, as did the rest of the world, through stories told in the media. It shook up my present in a way I could not have predicted.

On December 16, 2012, Jyoti Singh Pandey became the victim of one of the cruelest crimes any human can perpetrate on another. Jyoti means light, the kind of unwavering light usually found in candles and oil lamps rather than roaring fires. Jyoti is a steady concept, a light that removes darkness from its origin and emanates steadily outward. Jyoti Singh Pandey was only twenty-three when she was gang-raped on a party bus in India.

On that same December day, I had just finished organizing the Grace Hopper Celebration of Women in Computing,[5] India's largest gathering of women technologists. The event included India's first women-only hackathon and virtual streaming of the conference to fifteen states of India. I also organized the Women Entrepreneur Quest, which features six women entrepreneurs pitching their ideas to a panel investors, technology experts, entrepreneurs, and mentors. During this first WEQ, one of the women received $10,000, and this part of the conference has become a regular feature on CNBC India.

The event was all about empowering and inspiring women in technology to take on a broader role in creating and innovating. I had worked hard for the past seven months to bring it to fruition. Having succeeded, I felt at the top of my game. The conference was generating buzz on various social media sites, on television, and in prominent newspapers and magazines. Finally, women were finding their places and voices in India—the place I was born and raised and was given my first sense of the world. Yet, on the very same day, somewhere else in India, a horrific event was taking place.

---

5   http://gracehopper.org.in

I was still in Bangalore when the news broke. I cried when I learned of Jyoti's suffering. The news took me from the high of my success to a new low. I had just worked hard to empower and inspire women, and here—just a two-and-a-half-hour flight from me—was a woman who had suffered the most dehumanizing, horrifying experience I can imagine.

In an effort to determine what it all meant, I decided to go to the temple, as I often do when something has shaken me up. That day, however, temple didn't bring me peace. As I prayed, all I saw was various statues of goddesses being worshipped. Laxmi, Saraswati, Ambika, Padmavati—all women, all worshipped. I went to several temples that day—Jain and Hindu alike. Every temple featured at least one statue of a goddess where people were praying, worshipping, and offering fruit and rice.

Upon seeing this, I fell into deeper despair. How can a country that worships goddesses treat women as so much less than men? How can we worship feminine energy and rape the female form? How can we protect and kill at the same time?

Despite my excitement to return to my daughters, my trip back home was full of anger, sadness, and a fire within me to do something more. But what was that "more"? What could I do? I was—and am—part of the same landscape that so troubled me.

This experience of being both part of and apart from my culture was nothing new. As a child, I had seen female children sexually assaulted by the people they trust, people in authority; I had seen women struck by their husbands because they didn't bring enough property or money to the marriage from their dowries; I had heard of women in my neighborhood being burned alive in the kitchen and in-laws declaring the events to be "kitchen accidents." I had heard of women who jumped in the well because they were tired of their abusive in-laws and could not go back home to their parents because women in India are brainwashed by the old saying, "Once you go to your husband's home, you can only leave when you are dead." The women who committed suicide or were burned alive or were abused didn't have anywhere to go. No one would believe them, and some of them endured for the sake of those children. Jyoti had ignited a fire within me with her soft, light-like name.

When I returned home, I held my daughters tight. They couldn't understand why Mom suddenly had become so clingy, or why Mom insisted on getting a text from them every night to let her know they were safe in their dorm rooms. They had no idea about the world I was born into and brought up in. To them, what happened to Jyoti was the kind of thing that happens to characters on TV and others in the news.

By all appearances, I had merely returned to my life in Silicon Valley and had started to enjoy the fruits of my success from the conference in India.

Then, in April of 2013, something changed. Yet again, as I had when I was fifteen, I experienced firsthand the terrifying and soul-depleting cruelty of being targeted simply because of who I am.

I was at the Chennai Airport because I was starting to plan for another conference for 2013. My flight had been delayed before finally landing at 12:30 a.m. The driver sent by my Indian colleague to pick me up had left under the assumption that I wasn't coming. The airport was sleepy and lifeless. At that hour, there were no taxis to take me where I needed to go. My cell phone was dead, so I couldn't call the hotel to send a shuttle. Tired as I was, my brain felt like it was working at less than half its usual capacity. I walked out and tried to get directions to the taxi stand. An old guy who looked like the airport was his permanent residence wordlessly pointed me to the right. I trusted him and started walking. Ten minutes passed without any sign of a taxi. Then I came to a corner where I saw a group of men hanging out with drinks in their hands. A couple of taxis were parked nearby, but it didn't look like they were interested in my business—or at least not my money.

The group of men on the corner turned toward me. The streetlight overhead prevented me from seeing their faces fully, but I could tell they had marked me for a foreigner—which is essentially what I had become. I wore western clothes and carried a purse, laptop bag, and carry-on. As the men approached, something inside me screamed, "What the hell are you doing here alone? You need to get away."

I immediately turned and started walking back toward the airport. Behind me I heard, "Hello, madam. Taxi?" I walked faster and faster until I made it back to the old man who had pointed me toward the shady corner. I have never been so happy to see an obviously homeless person in my life. Rattled from my run-in with the men, I decided to stay at the airport until I could borrow a phone and get in touch with my colleague about calling my hotel to send a car.

Could you say I was paranoid? Yes. But, in the words of Andy Grove, "Only the paranoid survive."

Here was yet another experience that reminded me of my own limitations as a woman. Most of the time I traveled alone when I was in India, covering seven to eight cities in ten days before flying back to California. Organizing the flights this way was critical for me to get my work done and return home as quickly as possible to manage my one-parent-working household.

I did a lot of thinking on the flight back from that trip. I had already decided to pursue my dream of getting a PhD in women's leadership and had been accepted into a program. The decision seemed right. The experience I had during my trip to India seemed like confirmation of my desire to learn about and then contribute to the area of raising women's status in the working world.

During the next month, I took further steps to fulfilling my desire. I left my job at the Anita Borg Institute on June 21, 2013 and started my PhD studies in July. I felt ready to be exposed to new ideas. But there would be yet another turn in my twisting road.

I was only a few months into my PhD studies when my friend, colleague, and coauthor Suzanne introduced me to Pipeline Angels, an angel investing bootcamp for women working to increase diversity in the US angel investing community. I immediately jumped on the idea of investing in women-founded companies while learning about investment at a completely different level.

During this time, I began to realize that the curriculum for the PhD program was not what I had expected. I was interested in innovation, investing, and building relationships with the women leaders and mentors in this field. But most of the case studies that were part of my PhD program were about leadership from a western and men's perspective. I knew those were not the only examples, but they were what I would need to learn and write about if I wanted to be part of the program.

I made the decision to leave the PhD program—which many people told me was a mistake. I remembered my parents being advised not to send their oldest child and only son to America. What if they had listened to the nay-sayers? I wouldn't be where I am. I decided to do what I felt was right for me. Leaving the program was tough. It was also the right decision.

The day Suzanne and I joined Pipeline was exciting. Not only did I begin learning new skills, I started friend-ships with seven amazing women from different walks of life. Some of us are now writing this book together. Mixed with the excitement, though, was a good deal of fear.

Through Fear Toward Knowledge

Over the past decade, I had learned a lot about investing and made just about every kind of investment: real estate, stocks, bonds, mutual funds, insurance, and on and on. Yet I always thought that investing in new ideas and start-ups was something open only to a select few. At first I didn't even know how to make this kind of investment. Pipeline Angels seemed like exactly what I needed to get started.

At the start of investing through Pipeline—as at the start of this book project—I have to confess that I felt overwhelmed by some serious impostor syndrome. Who am I to guide others on investing when this valley is filled with people whose start-ups and investments have changed the world? Hearing or reading about some of the board members of the companies in which we are investing, I recognize how much I have yet to learn.

For a while, instead of motivating me to take charge and learn, those fears crippled me. When I first expressed this one day during the Pipeline training, my wise friend Suzanne assured me it is okay to feel this way and shared that others in the group felt a bit of that as well. So I took a deep breath and nodded. That evening, I journaled like a crazy woman. I wrote down all my fears and all my doubts. And then I wrote down all the things I would learn and the relationships I would build and deepen—all the people I would meet who would become friends, mentors, and colleagues.

The young women who have entered my life through my angel investing work are leaders, CEOs, entrepreneurs, dentists, doctors, lawyers, psychologists, architects, urban planners, and heads of public health and education programs. What a great way to connect with them, to learn from them, and, if needed and asked, to mentor them.

I have seen my fellow authors gain knowledge in a discipline that was new to all of us when we started. We all absorb in different ways and learn in different ways. We all have our own network of people, but what we have in common is the bond we have created because of our love for innovation. We all value a vehicle for investment that goes beyond the traditional, ROI-based model. We value understanding and interacting with the person who is behind the scenes, executing the vision.

My mom once said to me, "Only very few women in this world can dream and dare to execute their vision. If you can do both, it is not only your responsibility, but it's your obligation to do so." That message holds true now more than ever. We live in a world where simple rights such as reading and writing are not permitted to some women, child marriage still exists, and rape—and worse—is a common occurrence. So if you can dream it, then do it. My motto is "Dream, Dare, Do!"

Moving into the Future: Dreaming, Daring, Doing

One of the ways I have translated my motto into action is to look at how the leaders of an older generation, Baby Boomers and Gen Xers, can help Millennials[6] become leaders of our communities and companies and champions of the many causes the human race needs to focus on. They, after all, are the future.

The statistics are trending in the right direction for anyone who is a minority, especially women in the field of entrepreneurship and investment. Women are entering into and blossoming in historically male-dominated areas. However, we are not there yet, as my coauthors Geri and Suzanne point out in Chapters One and Two. What obstacles stand in the way for our next generation of women leaders? What attitudes and ideas might be left over from earlier eras that no longer serve them well? What does empowerment mean to them?

There are many ways to go about making an impact. Earlier generations of feminists had to fight to make their voices heard. Sometimes this meant a less-than-harmonious relationship with the men in power. I believe we have arrived at a point where collaboration with the other gender will take us much further than will working on our own. There's a saying that if you want to win, walk alone; if you

---

6   Here's a good definition of the generations: http://www
.talentedheads.com/2013/04/09/generation-confused

want to go far, walk together. It's not only about winning or going far—it's about both. It's about collaboration, where we create a shared environment—the new entrepreneurial ecosystem Suzanne describes in Chapter Two—so women who aspire to become technologists, scientists, teachers, CEOs, CTOs, designers, builders, or anything else can become just that. When women have the opportunity to align their work with their passions, they create innovative solutions that make things better for everyone.

The human race is composed of two genders. We need each other to not only survive but thrive and make this world a better place for all.

Women now in their twenties and thirties face different challenges and opportunities than those faced by women of my generation upon entering the workplace. There's more emphasis on having a career as opposed to simply a job. Like several generations before them, they will need to figure out how to integrate their entrepreneurial dreams with their relationships. (I use the word "integrate" intentionally; what used to need balance now requires integration.) They are entering an economy that simultaneously offers more opportunity and less possibility of long-term employment. They may be less discriminated against in certain contexts, but unspoken bias still exists along with often unacknowledged pressure to achieve.

Exploring the Future through Stories

I began this chapter with my favorite story, told by my father. I told you the story of how I arrived where I am, and the pivotal role played by the tragic story of a woman I never met. I'd like to end the chapter with the stories of several women who embody the importance of listening to your intuition and learning and doing what's needed to march forward.

The four women whose stories follow are part of a new generation. They worked hard to overcome barriers that remain to women achieving all that they are capable of. They are acutely aware of these barriers and they consciously work to "pay it forward" to the women who will follow them. Though their stories are different, they all arrived where they are through a combination of unexpected circumstances, passion, and hard work.

I asked each woman to talk a bit about her background and then asked them all the same series of questions. I am presenting their answers in the form of stories because I want readers to focus on the "why" that motivates them. What they shared with me offers not only a peek inside the minds of some successful women but also, I hope, inspiration for current and future generations—whether you are just starting out on your journey or have recently changed directions.

Sonia Gonzalez

Sonia Gonzalez is the cofounder and general manager of MdotM, billed as "Earth's Biggest Mobile Demand Side Platform."

Sonia had always dreamed of starting companies. She joined MdotM in 2009 at the request of Sourabh Niyogi, MdotM's cofounder and CEO. They had met when both were working at SocialMedia.com (later acquired by Living Social).

The start-up team was small: just Sonia, Sourabh, and Sourabh's brother. "His brother quit one week later to start his own company," Sonia says. "Sourabh focused on engineering and I focused on selling and retaining our clients. At some point, I told him that I wasn't looking for another job; I wanted to help build my own company." Based on the level of sales she had been bringing in and her contributions to the growth of the company, Sourabh made Sonia a cofounder in early 2010.

She was especially interested in the mobile space, given that it's a high growth, disruptive industry. The initial idea for MdotM came from Sourabh, but Sonia knew she wanted to help build a company in the mobile ad space.

The opportunity had come after many years of hard work and a leap of faith. She describes how her job as an inside sales rep at SocialMedia.com, which she took in 2007, was a step down; she had been in a sales role for more than four years previously at an international shipping company. "I didn't care... I wanted to work in a high-growth industry. I wanted an opportunity where I could use my skills and passions to impact the growth of a company. I also wanted to find a company where I could excel financially." At that time, social apps and sites were growing rapidly.

Though she felt a bit shy, since she was working with different types of professionals than at her first company, Sonia threw herself into her new role. "Every day, I had to tell myself that I was going to succeed and that I was courageous. I remember regularly repeating a Bible verse that says, 'For I did not give you a spirit of timidity but of power, love, and a sound mind.' I would say that over and over. This process of building my confidence is one that has helped me in pursuing bigger deals for my company now.

It's a continual process. Every day, I still challenge myself to think on things that are positive and empowering instead of dwelling on fear-based thoughts."

Perhaps this ability to build self-confidence arose from her roots. I asked Sonia what *inspirational* means to her and to talk specifically about her parents, whose own stories are the very definition of inspirational.

"To me the word 'inspirational' means people, places, events, things, etc., that give us the courage and strength to be our best and move forward in life," Sonia says. "The first and foremost source of inspiration in my life is having a relationship with God. I feel like I wouldn't be alive without a connection with Him. I try to read the Bible every day because for me it is where I find courage, strength, energy, hope, and inspiration to keep pursuing my dreams.

"I draw a lot of inspiration from my parents as well as other people in my life. My dad is one of the most hardworking people I know. He is now 67 and still works really hard. He's always had a relentless drive and determination to succeed financially." Her father, who sells produce wholesale, doesn't work quite as much now as he did when she was growing up. But during the busy season of May to September, he still often wakes before dawn and works past dark. As an immigrant to the US in the early 1970s, barely making minimum wage, he began selling produce on the streets and to local supermarkets as a way to feed his family of nine children.

"He has always been very supportive of my desire to start a business," Sonia says. He showed by example that if you are willing to put in the necessary work, you can pursue any dream.

"My mom is equally inspiring," she says. "She is a tangible expression of pure love. She's always been so selfless and giving, always desiring the best for her children. I remember growing up, there'd be times when we were scraping by and there was not enough money to buy groceries. She'd really stretch meals and use creativity to create something from whatever little or economical ingredients she would work with... She's equally if not even more resourceful than my father."

Sonia remembers that when she was nine or ten, her mom enlisted Sonia's friends to help sell bags of oranges in the streets, paying them a small commission for each bag they sold. When the washer or dryer broke down, her mother, who didn't know how to drive, loaded the family's laundry into a baby carriages and went to the local Laundromat. "She always manages to ensure her household is well fed and clean, even to this day as she approaches 68!"

Overcoming fear and lack of confidence is a thread woven through Sonia's story. "Authenticity to me means having the courage to be introspective and learn about your interests and passions." But beyond that, she says, you need to act: to take the steps needed to pursue those passions and interests.

"It's important for women to look deep within because I think we all have greatness inside of us." Sometimes that greatness is evident and accessible, and circumstances allow for it to flourish. All too often, however, Sonia thinks fear or life events cause women to bury that greatness. It can take a lot of hard work to draw out our potential, let go of the fears, and have the courage to pursue opportunities.

Sonia concludes, "I find that a lot of my women friends are held back by fears and worrying: fears of failure, fears of this, that or the other. My advice is to find ways to let go of the fears that hinder you. Do whatever it takes to let go—go to counseling, talk to friends, exercise, read books, seek God or spiritual help (whatever that may mean for you). Challenge yourself to see yourself living out your dreams, challenge yourself to be grateful for the good that is all around you. We often get so fixated on what's lacking that we fail to appreciate where we are and how far we've come."

Christie George

Christie George is the director of New Media Ventures, the first national network of angel investors supporting media and tech start-ups that disrupt politics and catalyze progressive change.

Christie was out of the country for the 2008 presidential election, but she imagined that she would have been actively involved in the Obama campaign if she had been in the US during that time. So, when she moved back from London in 2010, she was looking for some way to get involved in politics. Her journey to New Media Ventures began with that move, though she wasn't sure exactly how the journey would unfold.

"I didn't have any political experience," Christie says. "My career before business school had been in the media space. I learned about New Media Ventures through a friend." A small group of donors had decided they wanted to try to create something akin to a venture capital firm, but focused on progressive media and technology—and New Media Ventures was born. The organization turned out to be a perfect fit for Christie given her experience in media and her interest in politics.

"It has been an absolute privilege to help build the organization over the last four years. We have overseen investments and grants to more than two dozen social change start-ups—everything from Upworthy, one of the fastest-growing media companies of all time, to Ultra-Violet, an organization focused on gender equality. Our portfolio companies are inspiring and impactful, and we get to be part of building the market that launches them into the world."

Christie finds herself inspired when she sees people who are living their most sincere and authentic selves, regardless of convention. "It can be difficult to simply do things differently," she says. "The path less travelled can be rockier, longer and certainly more circuitous. But I am always impressed when I see someone taking it."

Christie believes it's important for women to discover their true selves and feels strongly that the world would be a more interesting place if we were able to hear, see and know the often invisible stories of women. The narratives we are most regularly exposed to—in movies, on television, in books—tend to be narrow when it comes to women. "The reality of women's stories is so much more varied and interesting than what we traditionally get to see. When women not only discover their true selves but also start sharing themselves with the world, it creates a snowball effect. Others start to see their lives being reflected back at them, and our collective narrative becomes that much more compelling."

Christie's transition from working in independent film in New York to working in technology investment in San Francisco felt simultaneously like a massive transition and an inevitable stop on a career-long journey focused on trying to answer the question: "How can we get more authentic stories out into the world?"

When she left New York in 2007, she had been at the same company, Women Make Movies—the world's leading distributor of films directed by and about women—for almost seven years. She loved her work there but was ready for a change. She decided to go to business school. This meant moving from a work environment comprised primarily of women to a business program that was more than 70 percent men. Christie explains another challenge. "Although I had been working on the business side of the film industry, I had never formally taken any business courses in my academic career. And as far as MBA programs go, Oxford's business school has a strong academic focus." She felt both challenged by the coursework and daunted by the prospect of finding kindred spirits in what felt like a homogenous environment, particularly early on in the program.

She ended up graduating first in her class, winning the program's Said Prize, and finding a large group of interesting friends and collaborators from all over the world along the way. "Coming into the program with so little background in finance and graduating at the top of my class gave me a stronger sense of my own capacity," she says, "and it broadened the scope of my ambition."

The environment of business school also prepared her to be "the only" in the worlds she would subsequently move in—technology and finance, which both tend to be pretty homogenous. "I am often the only person of color or the only woman in a room. But I feel comfortable in that role now and excited to be part of the solution in bringing more diverse leaders into the room."

Christie sees access to capital as one of the biggest obstacles for women. "The venture capital industry has funded an appallingly low number[7] of businesses run by women. This also makes no sense. Women drive such a huge percentage of household purchasing decisions; they are powering so many of the most trafficked sites on the Internet." Christie points to the post written in 2011 by Aileen Lee (Managing Partner at Cowboy Ventures, Strategic Advisor to Kleiner Perkins Caulfield & Byers) for TechCrunch: *Why Women Rule the Internet.*[8] "That post is no less relevant today."

Christie is interested in the creative financiers and entrepreneurs who are working to subvert traditional financing paths to support women founders. "At New Media Ventures, we are really proud to have a portfolio that is so gender-balanced, and we are continuously working on ways we can diversify our entrepreneur pipeline even further." More broadly, Christie believes, there are many spaces in which we need to diversify the decision-makers. Simply having a more diverse set of decision-makers will help accelerate women's success.

A first step toward overcoming these obstacles is identifying the places where bias and lack of diversity exist.

---

7   http://bit.ly/1w0iw9a

8   http://techcrunch.com/2011/03/20/why-women-rule-the
-internet/

Tumblrs like 100PercentMen and 2Male2Pale[9] show how homogenous so many companies and institutions currently are. Who Writes For chronicles gender diversity—or lack thereof—on the front page of the *New York Times*.[10] The Academy of Motion Picture Arts and Sciences provides another object lesson in how far we may still have to go. According to an article in The Guardian Online, "Although the Academy does not release demographic information about its members, estimates by the *Los Angeles Times* and Darnell Hunt, the director of African-American studies at UCLA, suggest the Academy is about 93 percent white, 70 percent male and on average older than 60. The Academy includes more than 6,000 people, each of whom is a member for life."[11]

When there is little diversity in the composition of a group of decision-makers, we can't be surprised at how little diversity there is in actual decisions.

"One part of my life's work has been about trying to address what I see as misrepresentation and underrepresentation of women's stories," says Christie. "This is what I was doing at Women Make Movies, working to distribute films about by and about women to demonstrate that there are *other* narratives worth noting than what we typically see."

But lately, her working hypothesis has evolved. Viewing women's experiences as a countervailing perspective to the mainstream may be totally wrong. "I would now suggest

---

9   http://100percentmen.tumblr.com, http://2pale2male.tumblr.com

10   http://www.whowritesfor.com

11   http://www.theguardian.com/film/2015/feb/22/diversity -protest-oscars-academy-award-ava-duvernay

that the alternative narrative, in fact, may be normative. We won't ever know because our existing cultural messengers simply ignore huge swaths of the population."

When women support each other, it signifies that women's experiences and voices are valid and valuable. And, in reality, in amplifying these stories, we may realize that the experiences themselves are much more universal than we originally thought.

Cheryl Contee

Cheryl Contee, CEO at Fission Strategy and cofounder of Attentive.ly, specializes in helping nonprofit organizations and foundations use social media to create social good.

In 2007, Cheryl caught entrepreneurial fever and moved to Silicon Valley from Washington, DC. Her journey to her new ventures at Fission Strategy and Attentive.ly began when she was passed over for a deserved promotion at a big PR firm. She decided to strike out on her own. "I quit my job and the next day sent out a tweet saying essentially that I was newly available—who wanted to work with me and do great things?" She got a number of nibbles just from that one tweet—which she sees as evidence of the power of a well-nurtured network of friends and colleagues— including a fateful one.

"A friend suggested that I team up with Rosalyn Lemieux, who was consulting independently," Cheryl says. "It turned out that we were yin and yang, a perfect combination of talents."

Lemieux and Cheryl wanted to help nonprofits embrace the possibilities of social media at a time when most still focused on e-mail outreach. Fission Strategy came out of this vision. The company now works with the world's leading nonprofits, foundations, and social enterprises to use the Internet in innovative ways to create global social change.

Attentive.ly was born a few years later. "We noticed that our clients were treating their social and e-mail audiences like two separate universes. We believed that they could be more powerful if they used the two together in more targeted and responsive ways." They bootstrapped Attentive.ly internally and then attracted more than $2 million in angel capital from what Cheryl considers "some of the most inspiring investors possible."

Cheryl tries to embody the word "inspirational" for her team. "People often say that *I* am inspirational. At Fission, I read an inspirational quote to our team every Monday and Friday. Studies show that cultivating empathy helps reduce burnout among those who work on social good projects." She draws inspiration for herself from positivity, hope, vision and determination. "Inspirational means to me a spirit that knows that miracles are possible if you are creative, resourceful and kind."

She believes that people often have an instinctive feel for authenticity—whether a person is just saying what their audience wants to hear or whether the person's statements are core to their beliefs and experiences. "Women in particular are always urged to smile and to cover their actual feelings in favor of pleasing others," she says. "When women are their true selves, femininity is no longer a cloak but a force for good that empowers others to reveal their truly powerful natures."

Cheryl discovered her own powerful nature through a process of personal and professional growth. Her experience as the founder of an A-list African-American targeted political blog—Jack and Jill Politics, which became highly popular and influential in the wake of the historic 2008 election—transformed her. "I achieved a kind of micro-celebrity," she says. The public notoriety and increase in public speaking created some stress. Despite the fact that she was already a professional and executive, "I had to reinvent my own self-concept from struggling minority scholarship student... to inhabit how others had begun to see me: an innovative and inspirational leader in both tech and politics."

Cheryl believes the biggest challenge for women continues to be balancing family and work. Men feel this pinch as well. The US provides the least support among developed countries for families—no mandated sick leave, maternity leave, or subsidized and readily available childcare. "As a society, we must prioritize family-friendly policies such as telecommuting and sick leave if we want to ensure that neither men nor women feel they have to choose between providing their highest quality performance at their occupations and providing their children with the best opportunities in life."

Because of this, it's vital for women to support each other. Women have to navigate life and work challenges that men don't always understand—even when they are fully supportive and well-meaning. "Most women take cues from successful women who are a bit older and more experienced in creating their own careers," Cheryl says. "I certainly did. Even when you are not actively mentoring younger women, know that they are clocking your every move. Act accordingly—how would you like to be seen in their eyes? How would you like them to pay it forward?"

Neha Bagaria

Neha Bagaria founded JobsForHer.com with the mission to reverse female brain drain from within the Indian workforce. JobsForHer connects women who want to restart their careers to companies looking for such experienced female talent.

In May 2013, Neha Bagaria found herself on a beach with a three-and-a-half-year-old toddler and an infant in tow, attending yet another wedding. "They were both down with colds, cranky and behaving like anything but the model children I had planned to raise," she says. "My reaction didn't help. I was blowing the entire situation out of proportion because I viewed their behavior as the end result of the last three years of my life... I realized that I was placing the burden of my lofty ambitions on the little shoulders of my children. I realized that it was about time I got back to being the person I used to be. It was time to restart my career."

She returned to her previous company and regained her confidence when she realized she could hit the ground running even after the three-year break. As her responsibilities at work increased, so did the quality of the time she spent with her children, husband, family, and friends. "I was no longer in a brain coma, no longer needy and emotional, no longer sweating the small stuff. I became a happier and more fulfilled person, which translated into becoming a happier mother and happier wife." And her renewed passion and intention to prove herself again helped her contribute at work with greater dedication and commitment.

Neha's personal journey opened her eyes to the many accomplished women around her who had stopped working when they got married or became mothers, or who left the workforce for a variety of other personal reasons and never returned. She started delving into the reasons behind this female brain drain. It became clear that Indian society needed to address many reentry challenges, from lack of flexibility and retraining opportunities to women's needs to regain confidence, overcome biases, and change mindsets. Neha continues, "It made me determined to enable other women to restart their careers and connect them with whatever they require to do so." She founded JobsForHer.com on International Women's Day in March 2015.

The vision of JobsForHer is simple: to reverse female brain drain from within the Indian workforce. JobsForHer connects women who want to restart their careers (post-motherhood/-marriage/-elder-care) to companies looking for such experienced female talent available on short or no-notice. The jobs on the JobsForHer portal range from full-time and part-time to work-from-home and project-based. JobsForHer also works with companies to offer Returnee Programs, which are internships for women getting back to work.

"In the three months since launch, we had one-hundred-plus companies posting job openings on our portal, including Dell, Future Group, Kotak Mahindra Group, Narayana Health, SmartOwner, SnapDeal, Sobha Developers, and Unilever, to name a few," Neha says. These companies have been rewarded amply for placing their trust in the fledgling venture. "We have been informed of candidates joining [these companies] in full-time, part-time, work-from-home positions, as well as returnee internships, often in the span of a week."

Neha's inspiration is, in many ways, rooted in her family. She is her parents' first-born child, which meant they pushed her to excel in everything she pursued. "True to their expectations, I stood second in Maharashtra in the 10th grade I.C.S.E. exams, graduated with honors from the Wharton School of the University of Pennsylvania, and decided to bring the Advanced Placement Program to India, founding my first venture, Paragon, right after I graduated and becoming the College Board representative of India."

As is typical, marriage moved her to Bangalore and resulted in the untimely closing down of Paragon. She then joined Kemwell, a leading contract manufacturer of biopharmaceuticals, where she became involved in finance, marketing, and human resources. She remained so inextricably connected to her work life that she couldn't imagine a day when she could be separated from it.

"That's when my first-born came along and a baby gave birth to a mother. For the first time, I became aware of the differences between a man and a woman. Suddenly, I became the primary caretaker of this tiny precious life and I was overwhelmed." The dedication and zeal Neha had previously focused on her work and studies, she now centered on her baby. "He became the focus of my being and I decided I wanted a sabbatical from everything else."

Her sabbatical extended from months to years, during which time she gave birth to a second son. Her perspective changed. "The second time around, motherhood seemed like a piece of cake. I realized I could do more and I wanted to do more. I [also] realized I had become a person I didn't recognize (or like very much) any more. I realized it was time to get back to work."

Neha explains that women's careers are an amalgamation of not only our professional lives, but personal ones as well, several times course-corrected because of marriage, motherhood, elder care, or for other personal reasons. But women are resilient. "No matter the obstacles, we find a route around them and keep going. Sometimes we might lose our way and feel that we will never reach the light at the end of the tunnel. But it is important that we keep persevering—even though this might not seem to be how we had imagined our careers would play out."

Neha's biggest source of inspiration when she restarted her career was Sheryl Sandberg, the COO of Facebook and the author of *Lean In*. In her book, Sandberg explains why the world has so few female leaders and candidly shares her own challenges in managing her personal and professional lives. She also makes a clear case for how and why women need to start "sitting at the table" and "leaning in."

"Her words have deeply resonated with me," Neha says. "They have made me realize that I am not alone in my work-life dilemmas." Women the world over face similar problems, like self-imposed fears and inhibitions, time-management challenges, and, perhaps most importantly, dealing with guilt. As a woman also on the journey of restarting her career, Neha faces many dilemmas every day that she personally needs to overcome. Reflecting on Sandberg's book made her realize how important it is that women support one another to succeed professionally and inspired her to found JobsForHer.com.

Neha found inspiration in Sheryl Sandberg's words about facing fears of all kinds, not striving for perfection at the expense of getting it done, recognizing that career paths can be circuitous, shifting to an "I can learn by doing" attitude, and not turning down opportunity.

"I have realized how important it is to recognize our fears and to name them; only then can we find a path to overcome them," Neha says. Whenever she is at a crossroads, she asks the question posed by Sandberg: "What would you do if you weren't afraid?" and uses it to help her stride confidently beyond her fears.

As women, Neha believes, we have a deep desire to achieve perfection in whatever we do—being a mother, daughter, wife, homemaker, and employee. "This puts us in a never-ending spiral in which we place undue pressure on ourselves... We need to remind ourselves that sometimes being good, and not great, is good enough."

It's okay, too, that a woman's career is often nonlinear and circuitous. We take on-ramps, off-ramps, and scenic routes on our career highways. "We need to stop deriding ourselves for it, or thinking there's no path back to the main road once we've taken a detour."

Women need to stop thinking they must be completely competent before undertaking something new. As an entrepreneur, you are constantly thrown into the deep end of the pool and need to teach yourself quickly how to swim. Whether it is expanding a business, ramping up sales, or finding investors, we need to remember that what's important is not whether we've done something before, but whether we have the ability to learn how to do it now.

Sandberg's final inspiration was, "If you are offered a seat on a rocket ship, don't ask what seat! Just get on." To Neha, this means women should "grab opportunities and fasten your seat belt. The journey ahead promises to be both exciting and challenging, and all you need to do is embrace it."

Every day since she decided to convert her passion and belief in career-break-women into a successful business model for JobsForHer, Neha has embodied the idea of doing great work by loving what she does. "And I've seen that with every woman who has joined my team." They are passionate and connected to the vision of reversing female brain drain from within the Indian workforce. "Strong women are those who build each other up instead of tearing each other down. It is critical that women support one another through the maze of our personal and professional lives, especially after critical life events."

My Future: Collaboration and Paying It Forward

"We can do no great things. Only small things with great love."

—Attributed to Mother Teresa

All my life, I believed I was born to do something that would change this world radically. Maybe I would invent a cure for a disease or patent a technology that would revolutionize the networking world—something crazy like that. I wanted to be known for *something*. I wanted to contribute by creating a solution for a problem that affects the masses.

Then I became a mom. Twice. As a mother, I realized, I held my whole world in my arms. That's when I decided that my contribution will be to do my best as a mother to raise two emotionally intelligent, kind, and contributing citizens of the world. That will be my greatest accomplishment. No matter how high I go in my career or whether I manage to invent a cure or obtain a patent, nothing will come close to being a mom—not just physically, but in all the ways I am present emotionally and as a role model for my daughters.

I kept working after they were born, balancing work and life as best I could. The universe must have taken my wish to be the best mom too seriously, because it gave me the life of a single mom. "Here you go," the universe said. "You love motherhood so much, you can do it all by yourself." Obviously, that wasn't the path I had in mind. Becoming a single mom caught me off guard. But since my daughters were nine and twelve, I have done my best to keep it all together, doing what I can every day to raise them. I certainly didn't have it all together all the time. I yelled, I compared, I cried, I felt lonely; I felt—and still feel—burned out at times. But I didn't give up the two things I love the most: being the best mom I can be to my kids and working as part of the changing technology scene in the San Francisco Bay Area.

At times, I wished I could stay home and relax, or attend every school field trip, or cook fresh meals, or not have to get on a conference call at 8 p.m. instead of cuddling with my girls. It was exhausting, but it was the most fulfilling decade of my life. When my older daughter graduated from NYU in May of 2014 and my younger daughter started her journey at USC as a freshman the following fall, I started reflecting.

Thinking about the challenges of those years as a single mom, I remembered some things that helped me. I'd like to share them with you because whether you are raising a family or working toward your own venture, you *will* have ups and downs. We usually ride out the ups smoothly, but downs can come after us with the sharpest and longest teeth. Here are three things that stood out as helpful for me in my journey.

1. I Learned to "Time Box" My Negative Feelings.

When I became overwhelmed by all the things that weren't going right in my life or how many things I felt I was doing wrong, I gave myself a time limit. I told myself, "Yes. I know it sucks. And you want to feel bad, cry, and stay in a dark corner. I understand that. So go ahead and do that for the next ten minutes. Be in your misery for the next ten minutes—but not a minute more."

After the ten minutes were up, I did one of my three go-to activities or tasks. I got on a phone call with someone I can depend on, I went for a walk, or I went for a drive with classical music.

Figure out your "go-to, lift-me-up" activity. Allow yourself a limited amount of negative time—and not more than once a day (meaning you can't spend the whole day having successive 10-minute negative time boxes). The limit is just one per day, ten minutes maximum.

2. I Established a Support Network and Let Them Know Exactly What I Need from Them.

For me, it was my two best friends in Florida. I told them: "When I am down, please remind me that I am doing one of the greatest things a human can do, raising children. Remind me that and whatever is bothering me, 'it shall too pass.'" This worked 80 percent of the time. The other 20 percent of the time, my friends just listened to me cry, rant, and vent. Then, after ten minutes, they stopped me (limiting my negative time box). They reminded me that my negative bank is out of funds. I will have to wait until tomorrow to go back to being negative. If I said anything after that, they would make lots of loud noise—even if we were in a public place!—so I had to stop.

Figure out who will be in your support network. Tell them: "When I am in my not-so-great mode, please help me by doing or telling me XYZ." You'll be surprised at how the simple act of connecting with another human being can help, especially someone who knows you well and knows what you need.

3. I Focused on the "Why" Behind What I am Trying to Create.

I use the idea of "end goals" and "mean goals" to help guide me. End goals are what you want to have achieved when you reflect on your life in your last moments. Mean goals are about what you want to achieve in the next three to six months. For example, two of my end goals are:

- Having done my best as a mother. I know I am not perfect, but I want to do this to the best of my abilities and not feel bad about anything that didn't work out.

- Having made a difference in lives of people who then can change other people's lives. That's why I like to work with people who are creating and innovating. I know their actions will change lives of other people.

These help me stay focused on why I do the work that I do.

Remembering the *why* can go a long way toward keeping you grounded when the earth seems to be shifting under your feet. In this chapter, I chose not to write about how to do things in the world of angel investing, about venture capital, or about being an entrepreneur. I wanted to get across the idea that no matter what role you choose, you also will be living your life. You will be playing different roles—mom, sister, wife, friend—and unless you figure out how your investments connect to what you want to leave behind in your life, you will be lost. My goal in writing this chapter was to reveal the importance of figuring out the *why* behind what you are doing. This aligns with my mentoring goal of helping Millennials—and especially women Millennials—connect with the *why* of their start-up or innovation ideas.

I want to make clear that your motivation does not have to be grand. You do not have to set out to solve world hunger. In fact, a modest goal may be better than a grand one. All that matters is that you feel deeply about your goal; that it matters to you.

I hope I have painted a picture of where I am in my life and how I hope to grow and prosper—and maybe to connect with some of you in the future. Thank you for giving me an opportunity to share important parts of my life, my dreams, and my challenges. The future is challenging for all of us, but can contain beauty as well. In the words that may or may not have belonged to Mother Teresa: If we all focus on doing small things with great love, we will automatically do a great thing together as a family, a community, a country, a company, and as humankind.

PART III:
What the World Could Look Like When Women are Fully Empowered

Many of the chapters in this book end with an inspirational nudge encouraging you, the reader, to take stock, get involved, make connections. In this final section, we offer some ideas about specific steps you can take next, depending on your goals. Each of our coauthors offers a concluding thought on what she believes is the most important thing you can take away from this book. We share our next steps and invite you to become part of what we hope to create.

Chapter Ten

Writing the Next Chapter in the Wingpact Story: Your Next Steps, and Ours

We hope you found a thread in these stories to connect you to a world you may not even have been aware of before reading this book. Now you have the power to step out and ante up, as Suzanne put it in Chapter Two.

If You are an Entrepreneur and Want to Pursue Angel Funding...

1. Create a business that you are passionate about. Don't compromise on your personal core values. The investor pool is diversifying, and you will be able to find investors that care about what you care about.

2. Seek mentors among the many organizations available to support women entrepreneurs.

3. Don't be afraid to challenge the status quo as the authors of this book—and many other dedicated women with dreams—are doing.

If You Have Decided to Use Your Resources for Impact Investing...

1. Look inside yourself and determine what you want your mark on the world to be. Then wield your money from that place.

2. Find like-minded entrepreneurs to finance. You are investing in the individual as much as in her company. In addition to confidence that she can build a great company, look for evidence that she will advance your values in the world.

3. Consider all the ways you can put your money to work: angel investing, crowdfunding, gender-lens investing, investing in a fund that supports your values.

If This is Your First Exposure to the Power of Women Funding Women and You Want to Know More...

1. The community to support women angel investors is exploding! Check out the resources in the Appendix of this book (Pipeline, Portfolio, 37 Angels, Manos Accelerator, Women First Enterprise, Wingpact Seminars), and the growing list on Wingpact.com.

2. Follow Wingpact on social media and by signing up for our newsletter at Wingpact.com. We will keep you informed of Wingpact events where you can connect with like-minded women, as well as inspiring happenings in the world of women's entrepreneurship and investing.

3. Contact us, your Wingpact sisters, (through Wingpact.com and social media) with your questions, comments, and thoughts. We have dug deep for this book, sharing our dearest passions and the tender hopes and new ideas whispering from our hearts. We hope to inspire rich conversations around the writing we have shared with you.

What We Would Like You to Remember

Suzanne: Don't Wait to Get Involved

Now—as in *today, this week, this month*—is a particularly exciting time to get involved in the start-up ecosystem around women entrepreneurs. A perfect storm of trends is coalescing to provide great opportunity for women entrepreneurs and investors. For me, the most exciting part is the opportunity to change business culture to reflect our shared values as women. Now that we can have women on both sides of the table, as founders and as investors, we have a chance to redefine how business is done. If we are mindful of the new business environments we create, we can have a far-reaching effect not only on the start-up culture in Silicon Valley, but on the scope of opportunity available to all people around the globe.

Wingee: Investing for Purpose Empowers Women

Women's consumer power has grown as we have come to control more wealth. Yet the *investing* power of women has yet to materialize. I encourage more women to not only work for their money, but also make their money work for them. One way to do this is to connect investing and purpose. By funding ideas that serve your purpose, you can make your mark on the world. At the same time, we must recognize that cultural, economic, and other biases that may prevent women from putting their wealth to work—or even from accumulating that wealth in the first place—really have no place in stopping us. Investing is impact.

Christine: Look Beyond Your Borders and Seek Mentors

My research into the experiences of entrepreneurs and investors in developing economies, such as Egypt, the Philippines, Argentina, and Venezuela, reveals how much progress these countries have yet to make in the area of angel investing. Yet because of this, investing in these economies has the potential for even greater impact. If you are part of a developed economy, consider the impact you can have by investing in these emerging regions—and don't be afraid to seek opportunities there. And, no matter where you are, seek out female role models and mentors.

Hana: Use Crowdfunding as a Stepping Stone

Traditional angel investing can seem complicated and overwhelming if you are new to it, and it does require a certain amount of wealth. The many variations of crowdfunding—donation-, reward-, equity-, and debt-based—provide opportunities for almost anyone who wants to begin investing. Crowdfunding democratizes the process of financial backing. It gives a voice to the creator/entrepreneur. And it allows supporters to show loyalty and backers/funders to participate no matter where they are based. It's a disruptive tool that is creating a new economy. The timing could not be more perfect as we tap the potential of women investors and entrepreneurs.

Karen: Get Comfortable with Money

Only when we are comfortable acknowledging what we have can we begin to put our money to good use. The long-standing societal taboo against women discussing money and recognizing our resources stands in the way of our progress. I came to angel investing post-divorce and with a deep desire to do something meaningful. Perhaps a major life transition will be the catalyst for you to act, too. But whatever motivates you, being able to honestly assess and discuss your wealth is essential for consequential action.

Jagruti: Collaborate and Lead with Your Heart

I want to inspire collaboration between and among men and women, investors and entrepreneurs, cultures, and people from different geographical locations. Collaboration is truly without boundaries and the only sure way to be successful. As we look to strengthen the world of investing for women, we will all need each other; having only women will be as bad as just having only men. Seek balance as you strive to level the playing field. And look inside yourself so that whatever you commit to doing will be something you feel passionate about.

Writing the Next Chapter in the Wingpact Story

As we worked on writing this book, hardly a week went by when we didn't hear of some accomplishment by a determined woman or gains made by women in general, from stories of women entrepreneurs to watch[1] to inspirational gatherings of women[2] to a reported boom in women entrepreneurs.[3]

Yet we also heard stories of old and continuing patterns of bias—and sometimes just ingrained habits—that prevented women from taking action to move forward. A study from the University of California, Berkeley[4] found sexism alive and kicking. *Newsweek*[5] reported that misogyny is alive and well in Silicon Valley. Stanford University[6] did its own research on gender bias and concluded that it affects women-led enterprises. According to Gender Gap

---

1   15 Women Entrepreneurs to Watch in 2015, Entrepreneur.com http://www.entrepreneur.com/article/241760

2   Women Entrepreneurs Rock the World in October, 2015 in New York City http://www.savorthesuccess.com/

3   What's behind the Boom in Women Entrepreneurs? TriplePundit .com   http://www.triplepundit.com/special/women-in -leadership/whats-behind-the-boom-in-women-entrepreneurs/

4   http://www.slate.com/articles/news_and_politics/uc2/2015/04 /university_of_california.html

5   http://www.newsweek.com/2015/02/06/what-silicon-valley -thinks-women-302821.html

6   http://gender.stanford.edu/news/2015/gender-bias-and -women-led-enterprise

Grader,[7] a gender gap remains in angel investing. A *Wired* article highlighted "Tech's Ugly Gender Problem"[8] with a distasteful anecdote in the first paragraph, and went on to say that "For every story you hear about investors behaving badly, there are far worse stories that many women wouldn't dare to tell." And Ellen Pao, a former partner in a venture capital firm, lost her gender discrimination case against Kleiner Perkins.[9]

Clearly, much work remains to be done. We need more economic opportunity for women, a fact highlighted by the National Older Women's League (OWL), in its 2015 Mother's Day Report.[10] One of the major impediments to women's success is lack of access to capital. And one way to increase access is to get more women involved in providing—and seeking—capital. Enter women angel investors.

To strengthen women's economic opportunities in a big way requires the involvement of women who might not previously have considered themselves able to invest because they lacked (or believed they lacked) expertise, money, or confidence. In this book, we have shown how women's own patterns can hold us back and we have shared our means of moving beyond our preconceived limits. To enhance your knowledge, we provided practical advice in a chapter on performing due diligence and company valuation. To reveal how you can make an impact even

---

7   http://gendergapgrader.com/studies/angel-investing

8   http://www.wired.com/2014/07/gender-gap

9   http://www.nytimes.com/2015/03/28/technology/ellen-pao -kleiner-perkins-case-decision.html

10 http://lionessmagazine.com/owls-2015-mothers-day-report -highlights-the-current-plights-and-successes-of-women-entrepreneurs

with small amounts of capital, we unpacked some of the exciting new trends in crowdfunding. And to buoy your confidence, we told lots of personal stories—both from the authors' experience as well as about other women entrepreneurs and changemakers.

The early chapters of this book pointed out that angel investing is about more than just writing a check. For us, impact is important (it's part of our name, after all). The way we define "impact" may be completely different from the way you define it—and that's okay. The important thing is that we, and you, continue to ask why we are investing. What motivates you? What's important to you? Do you want create a new path through the forest or walk along a path that already exists? Do you want to be involved in something, big or small, that has the potential to change the world?

We envision creating a worldwide network of women investors and entrepreneurs, a sisterhood that can help one another from anywhere with challenges as varied as how to get funding, where to find customers, figuring out what's needed in a minimum viable product, reading a balance sheet, or what to do when it seems impossible to integrate life and work.

Writing this book has been our first step. We have a long way to go. Maybe you are also just starting your journey, or maybe you are already many steps ahead. Wherever you are, we invite you to walk alongside us as we create a shared vision of the world we will be proud to pass on to future generations.

Appendices

Appendix A:
Digging More Deeply into the JOBS Act

President Barack Obama signed the Jumpstart Our Business Startups (JOBS) Act into law in 2012, requiring the Securities and Exchange Commission (SEC) to write rules and issue studies on capital formation, disclosure, and registration requirements. A number of these relate specifically to funding for emerging companies.

There are two parts of the act that are relevant to equity-based crowdfunding. Title II, Access to Capital for Job Creators, pertains to soliciting from accredited investors only, a practice already in place through platforms such as AngelList and Portfolia. Title III, Crowdfunding, pertains to general soliciting from unaccredited investors. This practice currently is not legal, but most crowdfunding platforms are gearing up and getting ready for the status changes.

Title II

Title II of the JOBS Act went into effect in September 2013. Founders who engage in Title II can now raise an unlimited amount of funds from an unlimited number of accredited investors through crowdfunding.[1] "Until the implementation of Title II, it was not legal for any private

---

1 Equity Crowdfunding 101: Is It Right For Your Startup? http://www.forbes.com/sites/ericwagner/2014/03/18/equity -crowdfunding-101-is-it-right-for-your-startup/

company, start-up, or small business venture to utilize social media platforms, e-mail, or any other public mediums to seek support around investment leads. Now there are no restrictions on from whom an entrepreneur can solicit as long as it is from accredited investors. The restrictions fall to who is permitted to invest, based on the regulations."[2] Normally, crowdfunding platforms take some measures to confirm that an investor has an accredited status because Title II requires that these companies take reasonable steps to verify that investors on the platform are accredited.[3]

With the birth of new industries comes the creation of services to support them. In the case of crowdfunding, companies such as VerifyInvestor have arisen to assist crowdfunding platforms maintain compliance with Title II requirements. VerifyInvestor markets itself as the go-to resource for verification of accredited investor status as required by federal law.[4]

What does this mean for angel investors? Title II is great for angel investors because it brings about more opportunities for angels to gain access to deal flow through an additional channel, the online crowdfunding portal. (Portfolia, discussed in Appendix B, is a good example of a crowdfunding portal.)

---

2 Crowdfunding moves to the next level: The JOBS Act's Title II and its effects on startup fundraising http://startupbeat .com/2013/11/14/crowdfunding-moves-next-level-jobs-acts-title-ii -effects-startup-fundraising-id3564/

3 Equity Crowdfunding 101: Is It Right For Your Startup? http://www.forbes.com/sites/ericwagner/2014/03/18/equity -crowdfunding-101-is-it-right-for-your-startup/

4 http://blog.verifyinvestor.com/

Title III

Title III of the JOBS Act relates specifically to equity crowd-funding and proposes to allow unaccredited individuals to participate as investors by allowing them to invest small amounts via crowdfunding platforms. The way the SEC proposes to effect this legislative mandate means that there will be two different types of offering under Regulation D's Rule 506:[5]

Rule 506(b) offerings cannot use general solicitation but in which nonaccredited investors can participate so long as they receive extensive information about the issuer of the securities, usually in the form of a private placement memorandum or PPM;

Rule 506(c) offerings can use general solicitation, but must be sold to accredited investors only, in which the market will let investors dictate the type of information that they need in order to make informed investment decisions.

Title III has been approved, but given its complexity the implementation details are still being worked out. According to Kim Wales, founder of the CrowdBureau, a few of the most pressing issues being worked out include:[6]

- Providing funding platforms with safe harbors from statutory liability

---

5   New Rule 506(c): General Solicitation in Regulation D Offerings http://www.crowdcheck.com/sites/default/files/CrowdCheck%20 Memo%20on%20New%20Regulation%20D.pdf

6   SEC Approves Title III of JOBS Act: http://www.forbes.com /sites/chancebarnett/2015/10/30/sec-approves-title-iii-of-jobs -act-equity-crowdfunding-with-non-accredited/#68d5c5486535

- Funding portal investor protection

- Increasing the investment size that would trigger a requirement for accounting sign off and full audits

- Rightsizing compliance requirements so that they scale to the size of businesses that will be using Title III crowdfunding

The fact that the SEC and the government are creating new regulations around crowdfunding and small business ventures demonstrates their significance as economic assets. With the implementation of Title III, the portals of investment for nonaccredited investors will open. This will allow crowdfunding sites, and those using them, to realize their true potential."[7]

---

7 Crowdfunding moves to the next level: The JOBS Act's Title II and its effects on startup fundraising http://startupbeat .com/2013/11/14/crowdfunding-moves-next-level-jobs-acts-title-ii -effects-startup-fundraising-id3564/

Appendix B:
Current Crowdfunding Platforms

This appendix provides a comprehensive list of the most active crowdfunding platforms that have gained traction in the past couple of years. None is a clear winner at the moment, but most of these sites are solid platforms where some existing venture capitalists and prominent angel investors have been experimenting as this space continues to evolve.

AngelList[8]

Since AngelList was launched in 2010, more than 2,000 companies have used it to raise capital and start-ups now raise more than $10 million a month on the platform. AngelList is not technically considered a crowdfunding platform, but rather an aggregator of deal flow and community of investors.

On AngelList, start-ups complete profiles listing information such as their previous backers and the amount of capital they've already raised. With those profiles, they can simultaneously pitch hundreds of certified investors—financial firms and wealthy individuals and companies. AngelList handles the regulatory paperwork (so start-ups have to fill out the relevant forms only once) and offers

---

8 Alicia Robb, PhD, Senior Fellow, Kauffman Foundation — Seeding Ventures: A US Perspective, 2014

resources for those that are navigating the funding labyrinth for the first time. A feature on the site called syndicates (similar to FundersClub's partnerships) lets users pool their money with that of a single well-connected angel. When that investor backs a company, so do they. Syndicates have formed behind some widely known Silicon Valley figures: Christine Tsai, a managing partner at 500 Startups; Kevin Rose, a general partner at Google Ventures; and Tim Ferriss, the self-help and marketing guru.

Lead investors of syndicates get to set their own terms. For example, Ferriss collects a 15 percent carry fee from his followers, a portion of any positive return they receive if the start-up is acquired or goes public. Ferriss has 485 backers on AngelList willing to commit as much as $2 million to any one deal. Start-ups such as the private taxi service Uber or the babysitting-jobs site Urbansitter, cofounded by female entrepreneurs Andrea Barrett and Daisy Downs, have turned to AngelList to meet new investors, get their deals done quickly, and add to rounds of fund-raising that are already in progress. Sprig, a San Francisco-based dinner delivery service, raised most of the needed $500,000 in a single day on AngelList, in part because investors using the site could see it already had secured money from prominent backers such as Brian O'Malley, a partner at the venture capital firm Accel Partners.[9]

---

9 *AngelList, the Social Network for Startups* http://www .businessweek.com/articles/2014-01-16/angellist-the-social -network-for-startups

CircleUp[10]

CircleUp is a curated crowdfunding platform that connects high-growth consumer product and retail companies with relevant accredited investors including angel investors, family offices, and funds. CircleUp mostly focuses on consumer products and companies in the food, beverage, personal care, pet products, sporting goods, apparel, household products, retail, and restaurant industries. There are no fees for investors and each investor is on the cap table[11]. Typical investment amounts are between $10,000 and $25,000, although some investments as low as $5,000 have been made.[12]

On the entrepreneur side, CircleUp provides entrepreneurs with the tools to focus on investors who are relevant to them. Companies that have used the site to raise money include Madécasse, a Brooklyn-based chocolate maker, and Ocean's Halo, a maker of seaweed chips. Since launching in April 2012, CircleUp has helped more than thirty companies raise more than $50 million in aggregate.[13]

CircleUp prides itself on being selective. It works with seed-stage companies that boast a strong team and a strong industry track record. Further, they look for companies with

---

10   CircleUp: https://circleup.com/getting-started/

11   A capitalization table or cap table analyzes the founders' and investors' percentage of ownership, equity dilution, and equity value of equity in each investment round.

12   Alicia Robb, PhD, Senior Fellow, Kauffman Foundation — Seeding Ventures: A US Perspective, 2014

13   Crowdfunding Site CircleUp Raises $14 Million http://dealbook.nytimes.com/2014/03/26/crowdfunding-site-circleup-raises-14-million

good financial performance, including high growth rates and strong gross margins relative to their categories. Considering that the retail space often attracts women, CircleUp provides a great opportunity to bring more female entrepreneurs as well as women investors to the investing table.

Crowdfunder[14]

Crowdfunder connects start-ups seeking funding with investors seeking opportunities. The companies on its investment platform have raised more than $120 million over the last two years, from a network of more than 120,000 Crowdfunders, including accredited individuals and institutions. The company focuses on seed and Series A rounds with round sizes between $500,000 to $3,000,000.[15] The platform has 33,000 registered companies and 10,000 registered accredited individuals, institutions, and venture funds and also recently closed a handful of deals in its first international market in Mexico.

The company focuses mostly on early stage investment deals that already have committed investors and first money in. Founder Chance Barnett describes Crowdfunder as "a serious place to discover the latest and greatest start-ups doing some very interesting things."[16] Crowdfunder's continued expansion will even the playing field for women who want to get involved in emerging markets.

---

14 Crowdfunding Site CircleUp Raises $14 Million http:// dealbook.nytimes.com/2014/03/26/crowdfunding-site-circleup -raises-14-million

15 Personal correspondence, Chance Barnett, Founder and CEO

16 http://techli.com/2014/09/is-equity-based-crowdfunding -right-for-your-startup/#

DreamFunded[17]

DreamFunded is an equity crowdfunding platform that provides highly vetted, prescreened start-ups to its more than 4,000 accredited investor members. Investors on the platform co-invest with successful, notable angels in the industry such as Tim Draper, Reid Hoffman, Brad Feld, and Mike Maples. DreamFunded has funded start-ups from the Techstars accelerator and co-invested alongside Shasta Ventures and Menlo Ventures. DreamFunded provides insider access to Silicon Valley no matter where an investor lives. DreamFunded is excited about the pending SEC rules that will allow everyone to make an investment in this asset class. And, through the new DreamFunded Exchange, investors will be able to liquidate their equity.

FundersClub[18]

FundersClub aims to democratize angel investing with its equity crowdfunding marketplace. They are one of the more innovative platforms, with features such as partnerships, where a lead investor with proven track record of at least one profitable exit is able to set up either a single-company microfund or a traditional multi-company VC fund that gets listed on the FundersClub site.[19] FundersClub allows

---

17   http://techli.com/2014/09/is-equity-based-crowdfunding
-right-for-your-startup/#

18   https://fundersclub.com/

19   *FundersClub's New "Partnerships" Let You Start A Venture Capital Fund Or Invest In One* http://techcrunch.com/2014/07/15/fundersclub
-partnerships/

investors to invest as little as $2,500.[20] The company also has implemented a new feature that will allow any accredited individual to invest in start-ups via a self-directed IRA account. (A "self-directed" IRA account means that the investor, as the individual account owner, has complete control over selecting and directing her own individual retirement investments.)[21]

Since late 2012, FundersClub investors have put $12 million into sixty companies that have since raised $200 million collectively—much of it from prestigious national investors. In February, the company released its first prediction of return on investment for funders on the platform: 41.2 percent. FundersClub tops a recent ranking of venture firms with the most momentum (based on predictions) by the research organization Mattermark.

Plum Alley[22]

Taglined "Where Women Raise Money," Plum Alley is an early stage company that began as a platform for highlighting women's technology innovations and entrepreneurial contributions. In 2013, Plum Alley introduced crowdfunding in response to the needs of a large number of its merchants and community members to raise additional money for their companies and ventures. Given the capital raising expertise of its founder Deborah Jackson, the Plum

---

20 *FundersClub fills void for startup investors* http://techcrunch.com/2014/07/15/fundersclub-partnerships

21 *FundersClub Incorporates Investing in Startups via Self Directed IRAs* http://www.crowdfundinsider.com/2014/04/36181-fundersclub-incorporates-investing-startups-self-directed-iras/

22 https://plumalley.co

Alley brand, and the strong focus on building technology, Plum Alley invested in building a platform that demystifies the process of raising money. Committed to "doing crowd-funding differently," the company's site presents the six stages of raising money and identifies the components of each stage to give women the best shot at being successful.

Plum Alley has showcased more than 100 women entrepreneurs since 2013 and offered them e-commerce to increase their customer bases. The company champions women who are building and using technology. In 2015, Plum Alley teamed up with Wealthrive to launch 1000 Strong, a first-of-its-kind membership program with a goal of increasing the pool of available capital and the base of investors who support women entrepreneurs.

Portfolia[23]

Portfolia is a crowdfunding platform focusing on early-stage consumer-facing products. This platform lets individuals and affinity groups discover and invest in private entrepreneurial companies in their areas of expertise and interest. Portfolia is particularly focused on creating a new class of women as consumer-investors by connecting companies directly to them and leveraging their combined buying power and substantial social reach to move markets and accelerate growth. Portfolia also seeks to reduce the risk and headaches for investors by listing only companies that have a lead investor who has invested at least 15 percent of the overall raise and has negotiated the terms for the investment. All follow-on investors get the same terms. Portfolia has strategic relationships with many angel and venture

---

23 Portfolia.com: https://www.portfolia.com/About-us.html

investment organizations committed to targeting female-founded and woman-led start-up companies, including Astia, Golden Seeds, Investor's Circle, Springboard Enterprises, and Women Startup Lab.[24]

WeFunder[25]

WeFunder aims to help unaccredited investors put money into start-ups and ideas they are interested in with investments as small as $1,000.[26] Although currently it plays by the existing SEC rules, the ultimate goal is to enable anyone to invest in start-ups that they find promising. Last year, WeFunder raised its own funding round, collecting more than $500,000 from about 60 investors.[27] Movie-ticket start-up Dealflicks raised $1.7 million on the platform.[28]

---

24 *Equity Crowdfunding Site Targets The Gigantic Untapped Consumer Market* http://www.forbes.com/sites/geristengel/2014/03/26/equity -crowdfunding-site-targets-the-gigantic-untapped-consumer-market/

25 https://wefunder.com/wefunder

26 Wefunder Raises $500K To Help Unaccredited Investors Put Money Into Startups http://techcrunch.com/2012/11/28 /wefunder-raises-500k-to-help-unaccredited-investors-put -money-into-startups/

27 *Y Combinator-Backed WeFunder Launches To Bring Crowdfunding Startups To The Masses* http://techcrunch.com/2013/03/19/wefunder -launch/

28 *Dealflicks Raises $1.7M on Wefunder: Startup Continues to Fill Empty Movie Theater Seats* http://www.crowdfundinsider .com/2014/07/45386-dealflicks-raises-1-7m-wefunder-startup -continues-fill-empty-movie-theater-seats/

Common Threads

A common thread among many of these crowdfunding platforms, with the exception of AngelList, is that they provide investors with a curated portfolio of start-up companies to invest in. It is in the best interest for all of these equity-based crowdfunding platforms to curate the best of start-ups companies for their own portfolio success and ensure achieving the highest levels of returns, both from the companies' fund-raising goal standpoint as well as their eventual exit. This is why crowdfunding sites carefully vet and select inbound and outbound start-up companies to be part of their platforms. AngelList, on the other hand, lists all start-ups, investors, and entrepreneurs without vetting, functioning instead as a matchmaker for investments and other types of interactions.

Prevalence of Online Investing Among Accredited Investors

A growing proportion of the roughly seven million total accredited investors in the United States are engaging with and investing in companies online. In this new market, new female investors are coming online and gaining access to investing in companies that they wouldn't have had access to invest in otherwise—without being a professional full-time investor or member of an angel group or venture fund—and often getting the opportunity to invest alongside more experienced funds in the same deal because of equity-based crowdfunding.[29]

---

29   *Crowdfunding to Narrow the Gender Gap in Venture Capital*
http://www.forbes.com/sites/chancebarnett/2014/11/21/crowdfunding
-to-narrow-the-gender-gap-in-venture-capital/2/

While the nascent area of equity-based crowdfunding offers great opportunity to level the playing field for both men and women, female angel investors are still largely underrepresented on these platforms. For instance, only one half of 1 percent of accredited women investors has invested on AngelList.[30] But, by acting early, companies like Portfolia are trying to prevent a worsening of the gender gap by engaging with both female entrepreneurs and investors communities on their platforms.

30 *Equity Crowdfunding Site Targets The Gigantic Untapped Consumer Market* http://www.forbes.com/sites /geristengel/2014/03/26/equity-crowdfunding-site-targets-the -gigantic-untapped-consumer-market/

Glossary

Thanks to 37 Angels (http://37angels.com/glossary) for allowing us to reprint their glossary of terms.

Accelerator: in an accelerator, a seed investment, usually between $15K and $50K, is made in return for equity. Start-ups are admitted in classes and work in groups. They are generally given a deadline to complete intensive training and iteration (typically one week to six months). Start-ups end an accelerator program with a **Demo Day** in which they pitch to investors.

Angel Investing: investing one's own money in early stage companies in exchange for ownership equity or debt. An angel investor typically invests $25-$100K per deal.

Bridge Loan: a short-term loan (up to one year) that a company uses in-between times when financing is needed. For start-ups, this type of loan is intended to fund the company to an anticipated future event, e.g. long-term financing.

Cap (Capitalization) Table: a table of how much stock ownership is held by each entity/person. Typically includes founder/investor equity and the employee stock option pool.

Common Stock: a class of ownership that has lower claims on earnings and assets than Preferred Stock. It is riskier to own common stock because in the event of liquidation, common stock shareholders are the last to claim rights to assets.

Convertible Note: a type of bond that can be converted into shares of common stock.

Demo Day: an event at which the graduating class of incubators and accelerators is given a chance to pitch to investors.

Dilution: a diminution in the value of holdings of existing shareholders resulting from the issuing of additional company shares.

Dividend Preference: preferred stockholders receive dividends before common stockholders. Dividend can be cumulative or noncumulative.

Drag-along Rights: the right of majority shareholders to force minority shareholders to join in the sale of a company. Minority shareholders will receive the same price, terms, and conditions.

Early Stage: the period in a company's growth defined by the evolution of its market development; early stage companies are focused on sales and marketing and on proving business viability.

Friends and Family: a common way for a start-up to fund their initial round of capital. A 20 to 25 percent discount from the next round is appropriate. The valuation cap is going to vary depending on the size of the raise and the size of the opportunity.

Fiduciary Duty or Responsibility: the duty to act solely in the interests of another; in the case of investing, the responsibility of an investor to make good investments that will earn a high rate of return.

Incubators: entities designed to support the development of start-ups through resources (mainly office space) and mentorship. Start-ups often stay in an incubator for longer (one to three years) than they would stay in an accelerator, though the lines between the two are blurring.

Liquidation: the process of selling a business's assets and using the proceeds to pay creditors when the business is bankrupt or terminated. Any funds left over are distributed to shareholders.

Mezzanine Financing: a blend of debt and equity financing requiring no collateral and not necessarily involving giving up interest in the company. This capital is typically used to fund growth or to enable management to buy out company owners for succession purposes. The interest rate is high, ranging from twenty to thirty percent, and lenders can convert their stake to equity or ownership in the event of default.

Preferred Stock: a class of ownership that has a higher claim on assets than Common Stock. In the event of liquidation, preferred stock shareholders have priority over earnings and assets and generally earn dividends, but forego voting rights.

Pre-money Valuation: the company's value immediately before funding. (For example, if the post-money valuation is $2.5 million and the company raised $500K, then the pre-money valuation is $2 million.

Post-money Valuation: the company's value immediately after funding. If the pre-money valuation is $2 million and the company raises $500K, then the post-money valuation is $2.5 million.

Right of First Refusal: the right to enter into a business transaction before others. For example, preferred stockholders have the right of first refusal to purchase additional shares issued by the company.

Seed Stage: the phase of a company's growth characterized primarily by product development. A venture in this stage is not likely to be generating revenue, but customers are interacting with the product. The business model is not yet fully developed, and seed capital is needed for research and development. This stage generates the first round of capital for the venture.

Series A: a company's first significant round of venture funding (though angels often participate in this round).

Stock Option Pool: shares of stock reserved for employees of a company. The option pool is a way of attracting talented employees to a start-up company; if the employees help the company do well enough to go public, they will be compensated with stock. Employees who get into the start-up early will usually receive a greater percentage of the option pool than employees who arrive later.

Subordinated Debt: a loan that ranks below other loans in the event of liquidation. This type of loan is riskier than unsubordinated debt because loan holders have claims to assets or earnings after senior debt holders are paid.

Terms Sheet: a nonbinding document that outlines the terms of the deal. Once the parties agree, more detailed legal documents are drafted consistent with the terms laid out in the terms sheet.

Venture Capital: capital provided to early-stage, high potential, high risk, growth start-ups. Generally, venture capital investments are made after the seed stage.

Vesting: a process by which shareholders (most often employees) earn stock over time. The purpose of vesting is to grant stock to people over a fixed period of time so they have an incentive to stick around. A typical vesting period for an employee or founder might be three or four years, meaning they would earn 25 percent of their stock each year over a four-year period. If they leave early, the unvested portion returns to the company.

The Four Stages of Start-up Funding

Stage 1, Seed Round: the first investment used for market research and development. Typically funded by friends and family and angel investors

Stage 2, Series A, B, C Round: rounds of financing from venture capital in exchange for preferred stock

Stage 3, Mezzanine Financing and Bridge Loans: can happen in-between rounds

Stage 4, Exit: companies can get acquired or issue an IPO by selling stock to the public

33889620R00158

Made in the USA
Middletown, DE
31 July 2016